Marinade
Magic
Cooking with Homemade Marinades

Other Books by Dona Z. Meilach

Homemade Liqueurs, with Mel Meilach
Macramé: Creative Design in Knotting
Creating Art with Bread Dough
Contemporary Batik and Tie Die
Soft Sculpture and Other Soft Art Forms
Ethnic Jewelry
Woodworking: The New Wave
Weaving Off-Loom

Dona Z. Meilach is the author and co-author of sixty creative books on a variety of subjects.

Marinade Magic
Cooking with Homemade Marinades

Dona Meilach

Contemporary Books, Inc.
Chicago

Library of Congress Cataloging in Publication Data

Meilach, Dona Z.
    Marinade magic.

    Includes index.
    1. Marinades.   2. Cookery.   I. Title.
TX819.M26M44   1981   641.7   81-65184
ISBN 0-8092-5967-2   AACR2
ISBN 0-8092-5966-4 (pbk.)

All photos by Dona and Mel Meilach
unless otherwise credited.

Published by Contemporary Books, Inc.
180 North Michigan Avenue, Chicago, Illinois 60601
Manufactured in the United States of America
Library of Congress Catalog Card Number: 81-65184
International Standard Book Number: 0-8092-5966-4 (paper)
                                                      0-8092-5967-2 (cloth)

Published simultaneously in Canada by
Beaverbooks, Ltd.
150 Lesmill Road
Don Mills, Ontario M3B 2T5
Canada

To Mel, Allen, Susan, and Richard

Contents

Acknowledgments

Marinade Magic is a more encompassing title than one would imagine. During the gathering, interviewing, culling, and testing periods, my life seemed magically touched by scores of people who were generous and sharing.

Somehow, I charmed my way into kitchens of fine restaurants, talked with chefs, and jotted down their "secrets," which, they assured me, weren't really secrets at all. Often, the only trick to reproducing restaurant recipes in the home lay in correctly reducing the quantities.

I spoke to cooking school directors and gourmet cooks who use marinades so routinely that they didn't realize that many people don't understand them and don't feel comfortable with them.

I hope *Marinade Magic* will change all that.

My special thanks to Beverley Stefanski and Susan Seligman and my other too-many-to-name cooking friends who contributed recipes, then helped test, taste, and suggest additions and deletions.

My husband, Mel, helped in so many ways—doing research and photography and serving as my most severe critic. He was just as quick at noting the failures as at licking his lips over the successes. When a marinade did nothing to change the flavor, he was the first to make me aware of it, and that recipe was scrapped.

I am grateful for the talent of my son, Allen, whose drawings illustrate the various chapters. He insisted he had to taste everything before he could draw it. Thanks, too, to Jacqueline Scott, who typed the final draft and appended several suggestions from her own cooking experience. It's nice to be surrounded by so many multitalented people.

Dona Z. Meilach
Carlsbad, California
June 1981

Marinade Magic

1
The Magic of Marinades

A marinade can make ordinary cooking extraordinary.

A marinade can enhance the flavor of good foods and add interesting tastes to bland foods. It can make tough foods tender and impart savory tangs to leftovers.

What is a marinade? It's an easy-to-mix liquid composed of oils, acids, and flavorings, in which foods are soaked.

With their simple combination of ingredients, marinades have nearly magical powers. They break down and tenderize tough fibrous elements in meats, poultry, and game. They impart flavors to many kinds of foods and preserve many foods. They introduce variety to everyday menus. And they help save you money.

What kinds of foods can be marinated? Raw meats, fish, poultry, game, vegetables, and fruits can be subjected to the wizardry of marinades. The results will be spectacular appetizers, salads, entrées, and desserts. Marinated foods can be added to and combined with other foods. Flavored vegetables will perk up soups. Marinated fruits are palate pleasers when added to puddings, pies, and cakes.

Marinated foods may be eaten raw or cooked. They may be prepared by every cooking method normally used: roasting, broiling, frying, and grilling. Recipes call for cooking on top of the stove, in the oven, over an open fire, in a microwave, or in a convection oven.

For centuries, countless cultures have used marinades in their traditional recipes for essentially the same reasons that we use them today. In fact, fabulously flavored foods from many foreign countries have inspired an increased awareness and use of marinades. Magazines and newspapers feature menus from China, Japan, Burma, India, North Africa, Denmark, Sweden, and other countries. Food writers and their readers try the recipes, experiment, and often adapt them to American tastes and available ingredients. There are new flavorings to find, new combinations to concoct. Marinating offers a foray into the exotic and a sense of discovery.

In addition to the new tastes and pungent aromas offered by marinated foods, there's another important benefit: marinades can help offset escalating food costs. Less costly cuts of meats and in-season foods bought at bargain prices can be tenderized and preserved. Market sales, or "specials," in beef, pork, lamb, and veal, for example, can be marinated and flavored so they rival the taste and texture of choice cuts. Abundant supplies of in-season foods can be preserved with a marinade and used out of season. Foods that lose some of their inherent flavoring, fragrance, and texture through freezing, canning, and other storage methods can be salvaged with a marinade.

The costs of using a marinade are minimal as is the effort involved. The last-minute cook may have to alter procedures slightly because marinades must be prepared ahead and foods are soaked in them for anywhere from one hour to three days before serving. However, tenderizing often reduces cooking time considerably.

TAKING THE MYSTERY OUT OF THE MAGIC

As with any kind of magic, once you know the secrets, you, too, can effortlessly pull the rabbit out of the hat. Marinating is an easy trick to learn. It's fun and gratifying, with dramatic results. Whether you cook for your family, a few guests at a small dinner party, scores of people at a banquet, or just yourself, adding marinades to menus can elicit awe, applause, and admiration.

In the simplest terms, a marinade consists of three basic ingredients:

- an acid, such as vinegar, wine, or beer;
- an oil, such as olive oil or salad oil; and
- seasonings—a wide variety, basically the same ones you use in any cooking.

Each ingredient has its own function: The acid breaks down fibers, allowing the oil to enter. The oils carry the flavors of the seasonings and add moisture to the foods. The seasonings stimulate the taste buds.

Ideally, a marinade should whisper and subtly enhance a flavor. It should not overpower the food. If all foods marinated in a soy sauce base tasted like soy sauce, rather than the foods themselves, the whole point of marinating would be missed.

The recipes offered are designed so that you may cook "by the book." But if you like to revamp and invent tasty recipes, feel free to do so. You can select a basic marinade, then by changing the herbs and spices and the liquid base, you can completely alter the character of the food. You can cook the recipe by any method you prefer. Marinades provide an endless vehicle for self-expression in cooking. With only a little experimentation you can perform your own alchemy and become a magician in your kitchen. From your shelf full of ordinary ingredients, you can magically transform everyday foods into memorable meals.

2
Marinade Basics

You can quickly graduate from apprentice to master magician as you learn how to mix and substitute basic marinade components: oils, acids, and flavorings. Your kitchen probably already contains all the ingredients you need. So wave your magic spoon, take out a measuring cup, and plan a meal for tonight that will be different and taste tempting—even though it may be the same food you had last night. Before you begin, you should bear in mind a few tricks of the trade so that every performance will be successful.

- Always place foods to be marinated in a glass, ceramic, enamel, or stainless steel container. *Never* use containers made of plastic or metal such as cast iron, aluminum, or copper. Acids react to these materials and may cause chemical changes, rust, and bitter tastes.
- Always blend the marinade ingredients well. Stir them with a wooden spoon, shake them in a jar, or mix them in a food blender.

- Foods to be marinated less than an hour may be left out at room temperature and covered lightly with waxed paper. For longer marinating times, store foods in the refrigerator in covered dishes so strong seasonings won't reach other foods. Foods that are improperly marinated for long periods at room temperature can be subject to bacterial growth.

- Always marinate fresh or completely thawed foods. Do not marinate frozen foods, as the thawed liquid will dilute the marinade. Wipe and dry foods with a paper towel before immersing them in the marinade.

- Foods that have already been marinated may be frozen *before* they are cooked. For example, if you wish to marinate enough meat to make kabobs for three meals, triple the recipe. Use only the meat you need for one meal. Skewer the remaining meat and wrap the individual servings and some of the marinade for brushing on during cooking in a separate package. When ready to use, the meat can thaw while the coals are being heated.

- The amount of marinade to use varies with the type of food. Some recipes call for completely immersing the food in the marinade. Others, such as beef, require less marinade liquid, but the food must be turned occasionally in the marinade so all portions are eventually immersed.

- Marinating time varies by food. The tougher the meat, for example, the longer the marinade period— perhaps as long as two days. Delicate fish may require only an hour to marinate.

- The marinade liquid may be prepared in advance and stored in a jar in the refrigerator overnight or until ready to use. This allows time for herbs and spices to release their flavors. Fresh herbs and spices require more time to release their flavors than dried ones. Use fresh ingredients for overnight marinades, dried and ground herbs and spices for shorter marinade periods.

- Usually, though not always, the marinade is drained from the dish before the food is cooked. The marinade may be reserved for basting or for thickening juices used for sauces and gravies. Older books suggest that a marinade be kept and reused, as long as it is strained and reheated every three or four days. Today, food chemists frown on this practice because bacteria can grow in the marinade and can have a deleterious effect on foods.

- Marinated foods may be cooked by any recipe given or by methods you already know well for a particular food. Marinades given for kabobs can be used in a baked dish. A recipe that calls for baking may be adapted for the grill, the microwave, or the frying pan. Generally, because the foods are tenderized, cooking time may be reduced by as much as one-third. Use thermometers for meats and poultry.

EQUIPMENT

You will need containers to hold the food and the liquid, perferably covered bowls of glass, ceramic, stainless steel, or enamelware. You will also need measuring cups, measuring spoons, shaker jars, knives, a cutting board, and perhaps a garlic press. A food blender or food processor is optional but handy.

INGREDIENTS

Ingredients for marinades should be of good quality and fresh when available. Dried herbs and spices, seasoned salts, extracts, and flavorings may be used, but remember that their shelf life is limited; they lose their strength after eight to twelve months. Salad oils have only a three- or four-month shelf life.

Acids

These include vinegar, wine, brandy, vermouth, beer, and other alcohol-based liquids, as well as lemon, lime, orange, grapefruit, and tomato juices. Acids also prevent bacterial growth and help preserve the foods soaked in them. Two or more acids may be combined in a recipe to alter the flavor, such as vinegar and orange juice.

Oils

Olive oil or any of the variety of salad oils may be used. Oils provide a smoothness and moisture to foods as they carry the flavorings into the fibers.

Flavorings

Marinades can be flavored by spices and herbs such as basil, coriander, thyme, rosemary, tarragon, parsley, cumin, and any of your personal favorites. Salt and sugar or honey have several functions: they impart flavor, heighten the flavoring of other ingredients, preserve food, and help retard bacterial growth.

The ratio of oil to acid will vary with the type of food. Salt and sugar are not always used. Salt may be omitted from some beef recipes because it tends to draw out natural juices. Many acids, such as beer, soy sauce, tomato juice, and catsup, already contain sugar and salt. Oils are not always added to marinades used for pork and some fatty fish, since these foods have ample inherent oils. Low calorie diet recipes eliminate oils. Low sodium diets eliminate salt.

Prepared salad dressings, such as French, Italian, and Caesar dressing already contain oils, acids, and flavorings. They can be used alone as a marinade or with additional amounts of any of the flavorings. There are prepared marinade additives containing mixtures of spices such as lemon and peppercorn. There are pre-packaged meat, fish, and poultry marinades that have to be mixed with water or wine. These flavor foods in only about fifteen minutes, but some are quite strong, so use them carefully.

The majority of marinade recipes are mixed as liquids at room temperature. Those that are cooked should be cooled to room temperature or chilled before adding them to the food. Dry marinades are a mixture of herbs and spices that can be rubbed onto foods that have natural juices that mix with the dry ingredients to become a liquid.

You can premix your own flavorings of herbs and spices and have them handy for easy use. You can make your own flavored vinegars (see page 15) and your own liqueurs (see Chapter 10). Homemade liqueurs are created through a type of marinating process and the products can be used for sipping, in desserts, and to marinate other foods.

When you prepare the recipes and discover you are missing one or two ingredients, feel free to use substitutes listed at the end of this chapter.

INGREDIENT REFERENCE LIST

Anise: a plant that yields seeds, roots, and leaves. Usually the seeds are available commercially; they yield a licoricelike flavor.

Beer: Any kind can be used. Beer is an acid. "Light" beers have fewer calories than regular beer.

Chives: herbs of the onion family with a delicate, mild onion flavor. Use them fresh from the grocery store or grow chives in pots on a windowsill or in an herb garden. The more chives are cut, the faster they grow. The blue flowers, as well as the cut-up leaves, may be used in salads.

Coconut milk: frequently used in recipes for marinades and sauces from southeast Asia. Milk can be taken from a fresh coconut or purchased canned. The coconut meat should be cut into chunks and soaked in water to cover. Squeeze out or mash the coconut in a food processor and strain out the milk. Freshly grated coconut can be used to garnish foods.

Cumin: a seed with a hot, bitter but piquant flavor used to season Middle Eastern stews and in chili.

Curry powder: a blend of cumin, coriander, cayenne, and turmeric. It is readily available and used in many recipes.

Dill seed: Dill has a sharp and pungent taste and is often used in Scandinavian recipes and in Middle Eastern dishes, sometimes accompanied by mint.

Fruit juice and grated rind: Orange, grapefruit, lemon, lime can be used. The juices add essential acid and preservative ingredients. Rinds add aroma and flavor. Citrus juices prevent bananas, pears, peaches, and other fruits from turning brown.

Garlic: a small vegetable that breaks into individual cloves. Always use fresh garlic cloves, if possible, rather than garlic salt or powder, which can become stale and impart an off flavor to a marinade. Garlic may be minced or slivered, or its juice can be used by squeezing a clove through a garlic press.

Hoisin sauce: used in Oriental cooking and marinades as a seasoning. It is a dark, rich sauce made from soya beans.

Honey: available with clover, orange, or other mild flavorings. (Also see sugar.)

Hot Sauce: ready-made or homemade. You may buy commercial hot sauces such as tabasco sauce or make your own by stirring together 1 tablespoon cayenne pepper, 2 tablespoons sesame or salad oil, and ½ teaspoon sesame seeds. When hot sauce is used in marinades, do not store the marinade longer than forty-eight hours.

Juniper berries: a purple-black fruit of an evergreen bush, available dried. The berries may be used whole or lightly crushed. They impart a sweet, rich taste.

Liqueurs: commercial or homemade (see Chapter 10). Fruit flavors—orange, pineapple, plum—are popular for marinades.

Mint: fresh mint leaves or dried mint leaves are often added to lamb and pork marinades.

Mixed herbs: sold commercially, usually as a blend of rosemary, basil, thyme, and marjoram. Other combinations are available.

Mustard: used as a flavoring in many of the marinades and made from mustard seeds. Mustard is used in two forms: *Prepared mustard* is available in different types, strengths, and flavors. Most of the interesting mustards are Dijon-style and come from France. Some contain spices that may be noted on the label, such as tarragon, dill, thyme, or peppercorn, and some are mixed with wines. German mustards are sweeter and have less bite than French mustards. *Mustard powder,* ground yellow mustard seed, is available as a condiment on the grocer's spice shelf.

Oils: Olive oil, vegetable, and salad oils are all used in marinade recipes. Oils vary in quality, taste, and price. The finest is *olive oil* of different grades, depending on which pressing of the olive was used. The finest (and highest-priced) olive oil is taken from the first pressing of the olives and labeled virgin olive oil. The lowest quality is made from the fruit and cracked pits. Olive oils come from France, Italy, Greece, Spain, and North Africa. *Vegetable oils*, also called salad oils, are made from corn, cottonseed, soybean, or peanuts. Recent newcomers to the market are safflower and sunflower seed oils. Generally, any oil can be used interchangeably in the recipes that call for salad oils. Olive oil and vegetable oils may be mixed half and half for economy. Oils should not be refrigerated, as they turn cloudy, but, if left on the shelf and not tightly capped, they can become rancid in time. Buy quantities proportional to your use of them over a reasonable period of time. Shelf life is three to four months.

Onions: For recipes that call for onions, any variety will do—white, yellow, or pearl onions. Red and Italian onions are sweeter and more decorative than white and yellow onions. Green onions, also called scallions, are fresh young onions with a small white bulb and leafy green top. The bulb and all but about an inch of the very top of the leafy portion may be used for flavoring. Chives, scallions, and shallots are types of onions with different tastes and one may be substituted for another. (See pages 16–17.)

Onion juice: Grate a large onion on a fine grater or chop in a blender, then strain.

Paprika: Often thought of as a colorful garnish, paprika also has a flavor similar to that of cayenne or chili powder, but is slightly sweeter.

Parsley: used for flavoring and garnish. The fresh parsely is preferred as it is available year-round in groceries and in gardens in tropical climates.

Peppercorns: Peppercorns are ground to make the familiar black, red, and white peppers, but there are many other forms of pepper: Crushed red pepper is very hot. Cayenne powdered red pepper is even hotter. Szechwan Chinese pepper is used in Chinese dishes and lends a reddish color. Green peppercorns are packed in water and may be used with marinades and added to prepared mustard for a zippier flavor. Buy ground pepper or whole peppercorns, which you can grind as needed in a pepper mill.

Salt: a basic component in most meat and vegetable recipes. Before marinades were developed, salt alone was used by sailors to preserve fish caught at sea. Salt, which is a mineral (not a spice or an herb), does more than add flavor; it helps other ingredients in a recipe to "bloom" and taste better. When used correctly, it opens the taste buds in the mouth and causes an increase in the saliva flow. It releases juices in foods in the same way. Salt intensifies flavor and, when used with sugar or sweet foods, it sharpens the sweetness.

There are several types of salt: *Ordinary table salt* is mixed with magnesium or sodium carbonate to make it flow more easily. It is fine and quite intense in flavor and should be used sparingly. When you double a recipe, it is not necessary to double the amount of salt. Use less salt in meat marinades, since salt tends to draw out juices. It is more important in fish marinade, as drawing moisture out makes the fish firmer and tastier. *Kosher salt* is coarse in texture and less salty than ordinary salt. It is pure salt with no additives. There are also *rock salt,* used with a grinder, and *fine sea salt,* usually sold at health food stores.

Shallots: are really the smallest bulbs of the scallions in the onion family. They are more pungent than larger onions, more delicate than garlic. As with garlic, only a small amount is used because of its flavoring strength. Freeze-dried shallots are often easier to find in mail order catalogs and gourmet food stores than fresh shallots.

Soy Sauce: a basic ingredient in many Oriental dishes and in all teriyaki recipes. Black soy sauce is dark, rich, and full bodied; light soy sauce has a more delicate taste than the dark.

Stock (chicken or beef): Use homemade stock with fat removed, canned stock, or bouillon cubes.

Sugar: White sugar, brown sugar, or a mild-flavored honey may be used in marinades. Sugar, like salt and acids, draws out flavor and prevents bacterial growth.

Tarragon: a fresh or dried licorice-flavored leafy herb, that gives a special tang to marinades.

Thyme: a garden variety herb that may be grown at home and used fresh. It is also available dried.

Vermouth: a mix of grapes, sugar, and aromatic herbs for flavoring. Most red vermouths are sweet and associated with Italian foods. Most, but not all, white vermouths are drier than red. Most French recipes call for dry vermouth. Dry vermouth and dry white wine may be used interchangeably. The same is true for red wine and red vermouth.

Vinegar: an acid component of marinades that helps preserve foods and break down fibers. Vinegars are the result of fermentation of an alcohol produced from the juice of fruits such as berries, apples, and grapes. There are white and red vinegars, white wine and red wine vinegars, herb and spice vinegars, and garlic vinegars. All these flavored vinegars can be purchased, but you can also create your own flavored vinegars using two different methods:

1. Heat 1 pint plain vinegar or red or white wine vinegar to boiling. Pour over 1 tablespoon of your choice of dried herbs or spices in a 1-pint sterilized bottle. Let cool and seal. If fresh herbs are available, use one sprig for each pint of vinegar.
2. Add herbs and spices in the same proportion as above to cold vinegar. Steep 4 weeks. Filter the vinegar. Rebottle it in sterilized containers and keep tightly corked.

Suggested combinations include vinegar with tarragon, dill, rosemary, basil, marjoram, or oregano. A clove of minced garlic or a tablespoon of minced onion may be added, if desired. If garlic is used, crush the clove and remove it after 24 hours.

Whiskey: Bourbon, gin, rum—all alcohol-based liquids—are acids.

Wine: Dry or sweet red wines, such as burgundy, port, rosé, and sherry, or dry and sweet white wines, such as chablis, and riesling can be used. When wines sit on a shelf too long, they turn to vinegar and can be used as wine vinegar in recipes calling for that ingredient.

Yogurt: milk fermented by certain bacteria growing under controlled time and temperature conditions. It is smooth, creamy, rich, and slightly tart. Marinades composed of yogurts and used on meats tend to break down the meat fibers, thereby making them more easily digestible.

SUGGESTED SUBSTITUTES

The following ingredients may be substituted for one another:

Garlic: Use equal amounts of shallots or scallions.

Herbs: 1 tablespoon fresh herbs equals ⅓ teaspoon dried.

Honey: 1 cup equals 1 cup packed brown sugar or 1 cup white sugar.

Juniper berries: Use equal amounts of red jelly or jam.

Mustard (prepared): Use equal amounts of dried mustard mixed with water, wine, vinegar, lemon juice, or milk to the consistency of prepared mustard.

Oils: salad oils or vegetable oils or olive oil or mixtures of half salad oil and half olive oil.

Onions: Use equal amounts of chives or scallions or shallots.

Shallots: Use equal amounts of scallions.

Spices: Approximately 1 tablespoon fresh for ⅓ teaspoon dried.

Tarragon vinegar: white vinegar with a touch of crumbled tarragon leaves.

Vermouth (red): Use equal amounts of red wine.

Vermouth (dry): Use equal amounts of dry white wine or sake.

Vinegar: Use equal amount of any other acid.

Wine: Vermouth or mix ½ water with another acid such as vinegar or lemon juice.

Yogurt: Use equal amounts of sour cream.

3
Appetizer Artistry

Appetizers set the stage for a meal, and when there is an aura of magic about them, all the senses are alerted. Marinated appetizers look good, smell delicious, taste superb, and convey a mysterious appeal that is hard to pinpoint. The familiar becomes unfamiliar and may cause you to furrow your brows and wonder what you are tasting while you smack your lips.

You have probably eaten many of the marvelous appetizers prepared by marinating: herring, rumaki, mushrooms, beef and chicken kabobs, fruits in wine, radishes in vinegar. As with these and many other dishes, you probably gave no thought to the preparation, but rather expressed an appreciative "ahhh," plunged your cocktail fork into another serving, and complimented the chef.

The range of delicate differences in hot and cold, sweet and tart, salty and spicy tastes is vast when marinades are used. You can subtly alter flavor and catch even the most sophisticated palates unaware.

In addition to often-used recipes, you will discover

several hors d'oeuvres from foreign cuisines. Do not let tongue-twisting titles frighten you. Many utilize essentially the same ingredients with only a few characteristic differences. Yet these differences are sufficient to make each dish unique. Dill, for instance, will be found in Swedish recipes. Olive oil is used in most Italian appetizers. Peanut oil is used in Eastern recipes. Soy sauce is indigenous to anything called teriyaki. A Hawaiian marinade usually calls for pineapple juice.

Perhaps the raw fish recipes will seem most exotic. We are not accustomed to eating seviche from Mexico or gravlak from Sweden. But, on the other hand, the natives of those countries may think we are strange for eating pickled herring, raw clams, and oysters.

Always remember to marinate in glass, ceramic, or stainless steel containers. Avoid other metals and plastics.

Minted Melon on Skewers

> 1 cup cantaloupe balls or cubes
> 1 cup watermelon balls or triangles
> 1 cup honeydew balls or wedges
> 1 cup Persian or Crenshaw melon cubes or balls or
>   any combination of seasonal melons

Minty Marinade:
> ¼ cup *each* crème de menthe, lime juice, white
>   wine
> 1 teaspoon poppy seeds

Mix minty marinade ingredients and pour over melon pieces in a bowl. Refrigerate, covered, for 3 hours. Drain. Thread the melon pieces on short wooden skewers and pierce skewer tips into half of watermelon shell placed upside down on a platter. Add mint leaves or other garnish in season.

Makes about 6 servings

Fruit with Wine Marinade

    1 cup pitted canned red cherries
    1 cup canned pineapple or pear chunks, grapes, or
        other fruit in season, diced into bite-sized
        pieces
    1 cup diced fresh or canned orange sections or
        mandarin oranges

Marinade:
    ½ cup dry red wine
    ¼ cup drained cherry juice
    ¼ cup grape or currant jelly
    1 tablespoon lime or lemon juice
    ⅛ teaspoon salt

Heat wine and cherry juice to simmering; add jelly and
stir until melted. Remove from heat and add lemon
juice and salt. Cool. Drain fruits and combine in a
bowl. Pour marinade over and cover. Chill several
hours. Serve heaped in cocktail glasses with some of the
marinade poured over the fruit.
Makes 6 servings

Plum and Bacon Appetizers

    12 fresh Italian prune plums
    3 ounces sharp cheddar cheese, cut into 12 ¼-inch
        cubes
    12 slices bacon

Marinade:
    1 cup soy sauce
    ¼ cup packed brown sugar
    3 tablespoons *each* wine vinegar and dry sherry
    2 cloves garlic, minced

Slit 1 side of each plum only enough to remove pit and
leave plum whole. Mix marinade ingredients. Add

plums and heat to boiling in medium-sized saucepan. Reduce heat and simmer 2 minutes. Marinate, covered, in refrigerator, 4 hours.

Just before serving: Place 1 cheese cube in each plum, wrap 1 bacon strip around each plum, and secure with wooden pick. Place plums on a wire rack over a baking pan to catch bacon fat. Broil 4 inches from heat, turning once, until bacon is crisp, about 4 minutes each side. *Makes 12 appetizers*

FRUIT APPETIZER VARIATIONS

Almost all fresh and canned drained fruits can be marinated in a compatible liqueur, brandy, or wine for 1 to 2 hours before serving. Always serve appetizers attractively with colorful garnishes for eye appeal as well as taste appeal.

Rosy Radishes

2 bunches large radishes, washed and trimmed
½ teaspoon salt
Water

Marinade:
½ cup oil
⅔ cup wine vinegar
¼ cup cold water
½ teaspoon pepper
¾ teaspoon salt
⅛ teaspoon dried onion flakes

Put radishes in a small saucepan with ½ teaspoon salt and enough water to cover. Bring to boil and boil 2 minutes. Drain. Mix marinade ingredients and place in jar with radishes. Cover tightly and marinate 2 days in refrigerator. This dish will keep in refrigerator for about a week. Serve in bowl or on platter.

Makes 2 to 3 dozen radishes

Marinated Mushrooms

1½-2 pounds fresh button mushrooms, stems removed

Marinade:
  ½ cup water
  3 tablespoons lemon juice
  1 teaspoon salt
  1 clove garlic, minced
  1 bay leaf
  1 small onion, sliced
  ½ cup olive oil
  1 tablespoon green peppercorns
  1 teaspoon fresh tarragon or ⅓ teaspoon dried
    tarragon leaves
  1 teaspoon celery seed
  ¼ teaspoon whole cloves

Combine water, lemon juice, salt, garlic, and bay leaf and heat to boiling in a medium-sized saucepan. Reduce heat and simmer, uncovered, 5 minutes. Add mushrooms and onion and simmer 1 minute. Transfer to a medium-sized bowl or covered jar. Stir in remaining ingredients and refrigerate overnight or for a couple of days. Serve on an hors d'oeuvre platter or on unbuttered thin rounds of French bread.

Makes 24 to 36 mushrooms, depending on size

Jicama or Yam Bean (pronounced *hick-ama*)

Jicama is a bulbous root that looks like a turnip and is indigenous to Mexico. It may be found in many West Coast stores. In Chinese food stores it is called yam bean. The root is peeled to reveal a meaty white vegetable that has a slight licorice flavor. It is often eaten raw in Mexico, cut into thin slices or cubes, or flavored with salt or chili powder and lime juice. It makes a delicious hors d'oeuvre and can be eaten with cocktail picks. Jicama is also used widely in salads.

    About 1½ pounds jicama (1 large or 2 small ones)
    1 large sweet orange, cut into wedges

Marinade:
    3 tablespoons *each* orange juice and grapefruit juice
    2 tablespoons lemon or lime juice
    1 teaspoon finely grated grapefruit or orange rind
    1 tablespoon finely chopped fresh coriander or 2
        teaspoons ground coriander
    1 teaspoon salt

Peel the jicama with a sharp knife or potato peeler and cut it into ½-inch cubes. Mix marinade, and pour over jicama, and refrigerate, covered, at least 1 hour. Arrange on a platter; garnish with orange wedges.
Serves 8 to 10

Marinated Cocktail Beets

    2 1-pound cans whole baby beets, drained

Marinade:
    2 cups tarragon vinegar
    4 heaping tablespoons brown sugar
    2 large onions, minced
    2 cloves garlic, mashed
    2 teaspoons dry mustard
    2 teaspoons salt
    1 teaspoon pepper

Mix marinade and pour over beets. Cover and marinate in refrigerator at least overnight. Drain and serve.
Makes approximately 48 beets

Marinated Artichoke Hearts

    6 large artichokes
    1 lemon, halved
    8 cups water
    Salt

Marinade:
    ½ cup olive or vegetable oil
    2 tablespoons *each* lemon juice and red wine
        vinegar
    2 tablespoons snipped fresh parsley
    1 large clove garlic, minced
    2 teaspoons Dijon-style mustard
    1 teaspoon salt
    ½ teaspoon pepper
    Lemon wedges (optional)

Cut off top third of artichokes with sharp knife; remove tough outer leaves. Cut off remaining leaves just above the heart and reserve. Rub cut surfaces with lemon half.

Heat 8 cups lightly salted water to boiling in large kettle; add other lemon half and artichoke leaves and bottoms. Cook over medium heat until tender, about 30 minutes. Drain on paper toweling until cooled to room temperature. Carefully remove choke of threads from each artichoke bottom with a grapefruit spoon and discard. Trim cooked leaves with kitchen shears. Cover leaves with plastic wrap and refrigerate.

Mix marinade in a medium-sized bowl; add artichoke bottoms. Refrigerate 2 to 3 hours.

Overlap artichoke leaves like flower petals on individual cocktail dishes and place marinated artichoke bottoms on leaves. Sprinkle leaves with marinade. Garnish with lemon wedges.

Makes 6 servings

Marinated Carrot Slices

8 to 10 large carrots
¼ cup water

Marinade:
¼ cup olive oil
2 tablespoons wine vinegar
2 cloves garlic, minced
1 teaspoon oregano
½ teaspoon *each* salt and pepper

Scrape carrots and cut into ½-inch slices. Steam or microwave with ¼ cup water until tender but not soft. Drain. Place in bowl with marinade ingredients. Mix well. Marinate in covered bowl or jar for at least 12 hours. Serve on an hors d'oeuvre platter.
Makes 8 to 10 cocktail servings

Rumaki

1 pound chicken livers
1 pound bacon slices, cut in half crosswise
1 small can water chestnuts, drained

Marinade I:
½ cup dry red wine (sherry)
⅓ cup soy sauce
1 cup canned beef consomme
3 tablespoons lemon or lime juice
2 tablespoons brown sugar or honey
1 clove garlic, mashed
¼ cup chopped green onions
½ teaspoon salt

Marinade II:
   1 cup soy sauce
   6 tablespoons orange liqueur
   2 cloves garlic, chopped

Cut chicken livers in half. Cut water chestnuts into thirds. Mix either marinade and pour over livers and water chestnuts in a bowl. Refrigerate 4 hours. Drain. Wrap a piece of chicken liver and a water chestnut with each bacon slice. Secure with a toothpick. Broil on a rack over a baking pan to catch the bacon grease, 3 to 4 inches from heat, about 10 minutes, or until bacon is crisp. Turn occasionally. Rumaki may also be cooked on a hibachi.
Makes about 16 appetizers

Zesty Shrimp, Rumaki Style

   1 cup cleaned, cooked shrimp (fresh, frozen, or
      canned)
   8 to 10 bacon slices, cut in half crosswise

Marinade
   ½ cup chili sauce
   ½ clove garlic, minced

Combine shrimp in marinade mixture. Cover and refrigerate 4 hours, stirring occasionally. Fry bacon slices until partially cooked. Drain. Wrap each shrimp in a bacon slice and secure with wooden picks. Broil 2 to 3 inches from heat until bacon is crisp.
Makes about 18 appetizers

Indonesian Satés

Satés are dainty, skewered, grilled meats often sold at public gatherings in Indonesia—similar to the sale of hot dogs at American functions. The recipe uses chicken, but pork, lamb, beef, or veal may be substituted. Prepare marinated skewered satés in advance and let guests cook their own over a hibachi stove. Serve with peanut sauce.

> 2½ pounds chicken breasts, skinned, boned, and cut into 1- to 1½-inch cubes

Marinade:
> 4 tablespoons chili seasoning mix*
> ¼ cup water
> ⅓ cup oil
> 4 tablespoons lemon juice

Sauce:
> Remaining chili seasoning mix (about 1 teaspoon)*
> ¾ cup water
> 1 tablespoon lemon juice
> ¼ cup chunky peanut butter
> 1 tablespoon chopped green onion

For marinade, combine 4 tablespoons of the chili mix with water, oil, and lemon juice. Mix well and pour over chicken. Stir gently, cover, and marinate in refrigerator 4 hours. Remove chicken from marinade and arrange on small wooden skewers. Broil or grill on hibachi 4 minutes on each side, brushing with marinade.

---

*Purchase 1 1½-ounce envelope of chili seasoning mix and divide it for use in marinade and sauce.

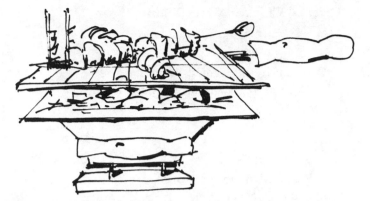

Prepare Peanut Sauce in small saucepan: Combine chili seasoning mix, ¾ cup water, 1 tablespoon lemon juice, and peanut butter. Stir constantly while bringing to boil and cook until thickened. Garnish dipping sauce with green onions.
Makes 8 to 10 servings

Broiled Sesame Chicken

　　1 to 1½ pounds chicken, boned and cut into bite-
　　　　sized pieces
　　½ cup pan-roasted sesame seeds

Marinade:
　　½ cup *each* soy sauce, sake or white wine, sesame
　　　　oil
　　1 large clove garlic, crushed
　　1 tablespoon fresh ginger, minced
　　1½ teaspoons sugar

Mix marinade and pour over chicken pieces in a flat dish. Marinate 1 hour or more, turning chicken once or twice. Drain and place pieces on wooden skewers. Broil for 5 to 6 minutes, turning once. Roll in sesame seeds and serve hot as an hors d'oeuvre.
Makes 4 to 6 servings

Oriental Chicken Wing Tidbits

    3 pounds chicken wings
    ¾ cup flour
    ¼ cup freshly grated Parmesan cheese
    1½ cups vegetable oil for deep frying

Marinade:
    ½ cup soy sauce
    ¼ cup Madeira wine or sherry
    ¼ cup *each* pineapple juice and orange juice
    ¼ cup packed dark brown sugar
    1 teaspoon finely chopped ginger
    1 teaspoon lemon juice

Remove and discard chicken wing tips; cut wings in half at the joint. Combine marinade ingredients in a bowl; add chicken pieces. Stir to coat well. Refrigerate, covered, stirring once, 6 hours or overnight. On a large piece of waxed paper, combine flour and Parmesan cheese. Drain chicken and reserve marinade. Roll chicken pieces in the flour and cheese mixture to coat. Heat oil in frying pan to 365° F. and fry wings a few at a time until golden and cooked through, about 3 minutes. Drain on paper toweling and keep warm while frying the remainder. Instead of frying, you may bake chicken in preheated 325° F. oven for about 45 minutes, then broil quickly on both sides until crisp. This recipe may be prepared ahead of time and warmed in the oven or microwave before serving.
Makes 18 servings

Peach-Flavored Glazed Ham Cubes

    1 cup cooked ham, cut into ¾-inch cubes

Marinade:
> 1 tablespoon soy sauce
> 3 tablespoons peach-flavored brandy or liqueur
> 2 teaspoons lemon juice

Mix marinade ingredients and stir into ham cubes until they are completely covered. Marinate 1 hour. Glaze under broiler about 3 to 4 minutes, turning with a spoon so all sides are glazed.
Makes 4 to 6 servings

Marinated Raw Beef Slices

Very thinly sliced raw beef "cooks" in a soy sauce and cognac marinade. The raw beef should be sliced almost paper thin. Ask your butcher to slice it on his meat slicer or freeze it partially and slice it yourself.

> 1 pound very thinly sliced beef strips, about 1½
>   inches wide
> 1 lemon, sliced thin
> 2 tablespoons fresh parsley, chopped

Marinade:
> ½ cup olive or sesame oil
> ¼ cup *each* red wine vinegar, soy sauce, and cognac
>   or brandy
> 1 large onion, finely chopped
> 2 cloves garlic, minced
> 1½ teaspoons salt
> 1 teaspoon peppercorns, ground

Arrange beef in a dish in layers. Mix marinade and pour over beef. Cover and marinate in refrigerator 6 hours. Pour off excess marinade. Garnish with lemon slices and chopped parsley. Serve with rye bread rounds.
Makes 4 servings

Mexican Snacks—Raw Sirloin "Cooked" in Lime Juice (Carne Cocida en Limón)

    1 pound lean ground sirloin

Marinade:
    1 cup lime juice
    2 small tomatoes, chopped fine
    4 tablespoons finely chopped onion
    4 to 5 chiles serranos, finely chopped, including
        seeds
    ½ teaspoon salt

Mix the lime juice into the ground sirloin, cover and let it "cook" in the refrigerator for 4 hours. Mix the remaining marinade ingredients into the meat and marinate 2 more hours. Roll into balls and serve with toothpicks or mound on a plate and serve with crisp tortilla chips.
Makes 4 to 6 servings

Brandied Beef Kabobs

    ¾ pound beef top round, cut into thin strips

Marinade:
    ½ cup brandy
    ¼ cup oil
    ½ teaspoon salt

Mix marinade and pour over beef. Marinate several hours or overnight in refrigerator. Thread beef onto short wooden skewers and oven broil quickly, turning only once, or let guests cook their own over a hibachi.
Makes about 24 appetizers

RAW FISH MARINADES

Raw fish plays a large role in the foods of many countries, probably best known are the sushi and sashimi of Japan. However, the Latin Americans are known for seviche, which comes from the verb *cebar*, meaning "to saturate." Raw fish is saturated or marinated in lime juice and other ingredients. The Scandinavians marinate salmon and call it gravlak. The Hawaiians call it Lomilomi. The French make a salmon tartare of chopped raw salmon, seasoned and served in the same manner as steak tartare, but with salt and pepper and dill. And pickled herring, which we are well accustomed to in this country, is marinated raw herring.

Seviche

> 1 pound *very fresh* fillets of mackerel, cod, sole,
>   bass, or grouper *or*
> 1 pound shrimp and scallops
> Parsley, avocado, or lime garnishes

Marinade:
> ¼ cup olive oil
> 1½–2 cups fresh lime or lemon juice
> 1 tomato, skinned, seeded, and chopped
> ¼ cup diced red onion
> 1 4-ounce can diced green chile
> Garlic salt and pepper to taste

Combine marinade with fish and mix well. Refrigerate, covered, stirring occasionally, until fish becomes opaque, at least 8 hours or overnight. Garnish with parsley sprigs, avocado slices, lemon or lime slices. Serve cold.

Makes 6 to 8 appetizer servings

Gravlak—Swedish Marinated Salmon

> 3 pounds center-cut fresh salmon, halved
>   lengthwise with backbone and small bones
>   removed
> Lemon wedges and fresh dill for garnish
> Mustard Sauce (see recipe)

Marinade:

> 2 teaspoons corn oil
> 4 tablespoons coarse salt
> 4 tablespoons sugar
> 2 teaspoons peppercorns, crushed
> 1 large bunch fresh dill, including stalks and
>   crowns

Scale salmon and pat dry. Moisten with oil and rub with mixture of salt, sugar, and pepper. Place half of fish, skin side down, in a large casserole that will hold it flat. Cover with a generous layer of dill.

Rub second half of salmon with marinade and place it, skin side up, on top of bottom piece with thick end resting over thin end of bottom piece. Add more dill on

top and around sides. Cover salmon with foil, then put board or large plate on top to weight down. Refrigerate 48 to 72 hours, turning the salmon over each day so it cures evenly. Baste with the liquid that has accumulated and weight down again. Before serving, scrape off dill and seasoning and garnish platter with lemon wedges and fresh dill. Slice salmon on the diagonal. Serve with sweet Mustard Sauce (below) and buttered rye bread. *Makes 6 to 8 servings*

Mustard Sauce:

    4 tablespoons seasoned spicy mustard (German style)
    1 teaspoon dry mustard
    3 tablespoons sugar
    2 tablespoons wine vinegar
    ⅓ cup vegetable oil
    4 tablespoons finely chopped dill

Place mustards in a small bowl. Add sugar and vinegar, then add oil drop by drop, stirring with a wooden spoon until sauce is the consistency of mayonnaise. Mix in dill. Refrigerate 4 hours. Serve in small bowl next to Gravlak—Swedish Marinated Salmon.

Lomilomi Salmon-Hawaiian

1½ pounds salted salmon, cut into ¼-inch cubes
3 pints large cherry tomatoes, hollowed out
Green onions or parsley for garnish

Marinade:

1 cup lime juice
1 large onion, minced
1½ teaspoons white pepper
¼ teaspoons *each* sugar and red pepper sauce

Place salmon cubes in marinade mixture. Refrigerate, covered, stirring occasionally, 6 hours or overnight. Stuff salmon mixture into hollowed-out cherry tomatoes for individual appetizer servings. Garnish with green onions or parsley.
Makes 12 to 14 appetizer servings

Marinated Herring

2 or 3 herring, cleaned and filleted into 2-inch
    pieces
1 onion, sliced
Sour cream

Marinade:

1 cup vinegar
1 tablespoon pickling spices
3 tablespoons sugar

Place herring pieces in a 2-quart glass jar or crock, alternating with onion slices. Mix marinade and pour over herring. Store in refrigerator, covered, for 5 to 7 days. Serve with sour cream.
Makes 6 servings

Mexican Marinated Fried Fish

1½ pounds flounder or other white fish fillets, cut
　　into 1½-×-½-inch pieces
1 cup flour
1 teaspoon salt
¼ teaspoon white pepper
¼ cup *each* vegetable oil and unsalted butter
2 medium-sized red onions, sliced thin

Marinade:
1½ cups olive oil
½ cup white wine vinegar
⅓ cup dry white wine or vodka
Capers, salt, and freshly ground pepper to taste

Combine flour, salt, and white pepper and coat fish
with flour mixture. Heat oil and butter in skillet over
medium high heat; sauté fish, turning frequently, 3 to 5
minutes or until golden. Place a layer of sauteed fish in
a 1½-quart baking dish and layer with sliced onions.
Mix marinade and pour over onions and fish; place
capers, salt, and pepper on top. Refrigerate, covered,
spooning marinade liquid over fish several times. Marinate 4 hours or overnight. Let stand at room temperature 20 minutes before serving.
Makes 6 servings

African Marinated Fried Fish

> 1½ pounds fish fillets (sole, sea bass, halibut, or a
> combination)
> ½ cup flour
> 2 onions, sliced
> ½ cup oil for sautéeing

Marinade:

> 1 tablespoon curry powder
> ½ cup wine vinegar
> 1 teaspoon grated lemon peel
> 1 teaspoon finely chopped mango chutney
> ½ fresh, sweet red pepper, chopped fine

Cut fish fillets into small pieces, roll in flour, and sauté
in oil until brown on all sides. Remove fish and cool.
Slice onions and brown in the same oil. Place fish in
bowl and sprinkle with curry powder. Mix remaining
ingredients and pour over fish pieces. Cover and refrigerate 2 to 3 days, stirring occasionally. Serve with
buttered toast or brown bread.
Makes 6 to 8 servings

Shrimp in Marinade

> 2 pounds cooked, peeled, deveined shrimp
> 1 cup chopped green onions

Marinade:

> 1¼ cups salad oil
> ½ cup white vinegar
> 2 teaspoons celery seed
> 1 teaspoon salt
> Dash tabasco sauce

Alternate layers of shrimp and green onions in flat glass dish. Mix marinade and pour over shrimp. Cover and store in refrigerator 12 hours. Stir gently. Serve in cocktail dish on shredded lettuce or directly from bowl with cocktail picks.

Makes 4 to 6 servings

4
Vegetables

There is something wondrously clever about the people behind the deli counters; they sell marvelously marinated vegetables. Why not? They are delicious and pretty. But the real secret is that they keep so well that if they don't sell the first day, they are still good the next.

Once you know how to marinate, you can have a greater array of vegetables than any deli; you will know all the ingredients are fresh and good. The traditional three-bean salads, the mixed vegetables, and the button mushrooms make dynamic dinner accompaniments. They are particularly welcome at buffets. Marinated vegetables are soft and pliable, easy to cut and eat with only a fork.

Flavor, appearance, and convenience are only a part of the bounty you get when you soak vegetables in wines and vinegars rather than splashing them with a dressing. The many variations on niçoise salads are the results of marinating vegetables in French dressing. Pickling, a first cousin to marinating, enables us to buy large quantities of in-season vegetables and preserve them for out-of-season treats.

Marinade ingredients should be mixed thoroughly before adding them to the vegetables. Then refrigerate all together in a covered glass or ceramic bowl for at least an hour. Fibrous vegetables such as beans, peas, tomatoes, carrots, cucumbers, zucchini, artichokes, mushrooms, asparagus, and broccoli are best for marinating. Vegetables may be marinated raw or cooked.

Try the combinations suggested in this chapter, then use your marinade magic to make medleys and mixtures of your own. Switch and substitute your favorite ingredients both in the vegetables and in the marinades.

Drain and reserve marinated vegetable juices before serving. Then freeze or refrigerate the juices and use them in soups. The juices contain abundant vegetable minerals and vitamins and the flavor is mild because the vegetables have absorbed most of the vinegar.

Western-Style Cole Slaw

    4 cups finely chopped white or red cabbage
    1 cup *each* green pepper and celery, diced

Marinade:
    1 cup *each* mild flavored honey and wine vinegar
    ½ cup finely chopped onion
    1 teaspoon *each* salt and celery seed

Mix marinade in small pan, bring to boil, reduce heat, and simmer 5 minutes. Cool. Pour over vegetables and toss lightly. Cover and refrigerate several hours or overnight to blend flavors.

Makes 8 to 10 servings

Avocado Salad

> 2 medium-sized ripe avocados
> ½ Bermuda onion, sliced paper thin
> 1 orange
> Shredded lettuce

Marinade:

> ½ cup salad oil
> 3 tablespoons wine vinegar
> 3 tablespoons lemon juice
> ½ teaspoon sugar
> ⅛ teaspoon *each* salt and pepper

Peel avocados and cut into cubes. Place in bowl with onion. Mix marinade and pour over vegetables. Cover and refrigerate several hours, stirring occasionally. Just before serving, peel and section orange, add to salad, and toss lightly. Serve on a bed of shredded lettuce.
Makes 4 servings

Eggplant

>1 unpeeled eggplant, cut into 1-inch cubes
>Salted water
>¾ cup olive oil

Marinade:

>½ cup wine vinegar
>1 clove garlic, mashed
>1 teaspoon *each* oregano and salt
>½ teaspoon *each* sweet basil and pepper
>1 teaspoon fresh dill (optional)

Boil eggplant in salted water to cover until cubes are soft but retain their shape, about 10 minutes. Drain. Combine marinade ingredients, adding dill if you prefer a Scandinavian flavor, and pour marinade over eggplant in bowl. Cover and refrigerate 8 hours or overnight. Just before serving, toss with oil.

Makes 6 to 8 servings

Tomatoes

3 large tomatoes, sliced

Marinade:

¼ cup olive or salad oil
1 tablespoon *each* tarragon vinegar and red wine
     vinegar
1 clove garlic, crushed
¼ cup chopped parsley
2 teaspoons Dijon-style mustard
1 teaspoon *each* salt and sugar
¼ teaspoon pepper

Cut tomatoes into ½-inch slices and rearrange in tomato shape in bowl. Mix marinade in covered jar and shake well to blend. Pour over tomatoes. Cover lightly and refrigerate 2 hours. Let stand at room temperature 20 minutes before serving.
Makes 5 to 6 servings

Whole String Beans Niçoise

   2 16-ounce cans whole string beans
   1 teaspoon *each* sweet basil and ground pepper
   Lettuce

*Marinade:**

   2 tablespoons wine vinegar
   6 tablespoons olive oil
   1 tablespoon fresh lemon juice
   1 teaspoon salt
   ½ teaspoon black pepper, coarsely ground
   1 clove garlic, pressed

Combine marinade ingredients in a large jar and shake well to blend. Drain beans and spread a layer in an 8″ × 8″ glass baking dish. Cover with a layer of marinade and sprinkle with sweet basil and pepper. Repeat layers. Cover and refrigerate overnight, turning gently to keep ingredients covered with liquid. Drain excess dressing and serve beans on a bed of lettuce.
Makes 4 to 6 servings

French-Cut String Beans with Bacon and Wine

   1 pound fresh or frozen string beans, cut French-
      style
   6 slices bacon
   1 medium-sized onion, cut into narrow wedges
   1 teaspoon Dijon-style mustard
   Salt and pepper to taste

Marinade:

   ½ cup *each* cider vinegar and dry white wine
   ⅓ cup salad oil
   ¼ cup sugar

*You may substitute 1 cup prepared French dressing for the marinade, if desired.

Prepare beans and cook in lightly salted water until tender. Drain and place beans in a bowl. Cut bacon into strips about ⅛ inch wide. Fry in saucepan over moderate heat, stirring frequently, until light brown. Remove bacon from pan. Sauté onion wedges in bacon grease and stir until tender.

Mix marinade ingredients and add to onion in pan. Slowly bring liquid to a boil, scraping bottom of pan with a wooden spoon. Simmer 3 minutes. Stir in mustard until well blended. Pour liquid over string beans. Add bacon, salt, and pepper. Marinate in refrigerator overnight. Serve in deep salad dishes.

Makes 4 servings

Basic Three-Bean Salad

> 1 16-ounce can *each* cut green beans, cut wax
>   beans, and kidney beans
> 1 red or white onion, sliced and separated into
>   rings
> 1 green pepper, sliced
> Lettuce (optional)

Marinade:
> ⅔ cup vinegar
> ⅓ cup salad oil
> ¾ cup sugar
> 1 teaspoon *each* salt and pepper
> ½ teaspoon oregano

Drain beans and discard liquid. Combine beans with onions and green pepper in bowl and pour marinade over them. Refrigerate overnight. To serve, toss to coat well with marinade, then drain thoroughly and serve in dishes or on a bed of lettuce.

Makes 6 to 8 servings

Indonesian Atjar Biet (Sweet-Sour Beets)

1 to 1½ (1 pound) cans sliced beets, drained

Marinade:
1 10½-ounce can beef bouillon or 1¼ cup made
    from 2 cubes
¾ cup white vinegar
2 tablespoons sugar
2 teaspoons *each* whole cloves and peppercorns

Place beef bouillon in a saucepan and add other marinade ingredients. Bring to a boil, remove from heat, and add beets. Let stand several hours or overnight. Drain and serve.

Note: Fresh beets may be used instead of canned. Boil cleaned beets in spice mixture until tender. Remove beets and slice, then replace in spice mixture and marinate as above.

Makes 4 to 6 servings

Carrots in Pickle Brine

1–1½ cups sweet pickle brine, left over from jar
    pickles
2 sprigs parsley
1 thin slice fresh lemon
1–2 bunches baby carrots, 3–4 inches long,
    scrubbed but not peeled

Heat pickle brine, parsley, and lemon to boiling. Drop carrots in and continue to simmer for about 5 minutes until carrots are heated through but still crisp. Cool. Store in refrigerator in covered glass container for 4 to 6 hours or until thoroughly chilled.

Makes 6 to 8 servings

North African Cucumbers

2 large cucumbers, pared, halved lengthwise, and
cut into 1-inch pieces
Parsley sprigs
Paprika

Marinade:
2 tablespoons vegetable oil
3 tablespoons red wine vinegar
½ teaspoon *each* dried thyme leaves and salt
¼ teaspoon *each* dried oregano and dried marjoram
leaves

Mix marinade. Pour over cucumbers and refrigerate
overnight. Drain off marinade. Decorate with parsely
and sprinkle with paprika for color.
Makes 6 servings

Cucumbers in Dilled Sour Cream

3 cucumbers, pared and sliced thin
1 yellow onion, sliced thin

Marinade:
1 part vinegar and 1 part water—enough to cover
cucumbers
1 tablespoon sugar
Salt and pepper to taste
2 cups sour cream
2 tablespoons *each* lemon juice and tarragon vinegar
½ teaspoon fresh dill
2 green onions, finely chopped

Mix vinegar, water, sugar, salt, and pepper for preliminary marinade. Pour over cucumbers and sliced onions and refrigerate 2 hours. Drain thoroughly.

Mix remaining ingredients together and gently stir in the drained cucumbers. Chill until ready to serve. May be prepared early in the day.

Makes 6 servings as a side dish

Danish Cucumbers

> 3 large cucumbers, peeled and sliced thin
> 1 tablespoon salt

Marinade:

> ⅓ cup white vinegar, white wine, or cider vinegar
> 1½ teaspoons sugar
> ¼ teaspoon pepper

Lay cucumbers on one plate and cover with salt. Place another plate on top of the cucumbers as a weight; this draws out the juices. Let stand 1 hour at room temperature or overnight in refrigerator. Put cucumbers in strainer or colander. Drain off juices and lightly rinse off salt with cold water. Put cucumbers in bowl, add marinade, and let stand 2 hours.

Makes 6 servings as a side dish

Lettuce, Spinach, Orange Salad

> 1 medium head iceberg or romaine lettuce
> 2 cups spinach leaves
> 2 tangerines or oranges, peeled and sectioned
> ½ cup onion rings

Marinade:

> 3 tablespoons salad oil
> 2 tablespoons *each* vinegar and corn syrup
> ½ teaspoon seasoned salt
> ¼ teaspoon *each* celery seed and dill seed
> ⅛ teaspoon pepper

Tear lettuce and spinach leaves into bite-sized pieces. Cut each tangerine or orange section in half. Mix marinade and pour over fruit and onion rings in small bowl and marinate for 30 minutes. Just before serving, pour mixture over greens and toss.

For a luncheon salad: Add 1 15-ounce can tuna, drained and broken, or 2 cups cooked diced chicken to tangerines and onions. Marinate.

Makes 4 servings

Nutty Salad

  ¼ cup broken walnuts
  2 tomatoes, peeled and cut into chunks
  1 cucumber, pared and sliced thin
  1 cup celery
  1 onion, sliced and separated into rings
  4 tablespoons sliced, pitted green or black olives
  Shredded lettuce

Marinade:
  ½ cup vinegar
  4 tablespoons salad oil or olive oil
  ½ teaspoon salt
  ¼ teaspoon *each* pepper and crushed oregano

Mix marinade ingredients thoroughly and pour over nuts and all vegetables except lettuce. Toss well. Cover and refrigerate 1½ hours, tossing occasionally. Drain before serving or use a slotted spoon and serve salad on a bed of shredded lettuce.

Makes 4 to 6 servings

Zucchini and Mushrooms

  ½ pound mushrooms, sliced thin
  ½ pound small zucchini, sliced thin
  2 tablespoons *each* chopped pimiento and chopped
    parsley

Marinade:
 ¼ cup salad oil
 ⅓ cup tarragon vinegar
 2 tablespoons lemon or lime juice
 2 tablespoons brandy
 1¼ teaspoons onion salt
 ½ teaspoon sugar
 ¼ teaspoon *each* white pepper and crumbled basil
 ⅛ teaspoon *each* fresh dill weed and paprika
 3 drops hot pepper sauce

Combine marinade ingredients and mix thoroughly in a small jar. Pour over sliced mushrooms and zucchini and mix gently. Chill 1 hour. Garnish with pimiento and parsley before serving.
Makes 6 to 8 servings

Minted Zucchini

 2 medium-sized zucchini, sliced thin
 ¼ cup salad oil

Marinade:
 ½ cup vinegar
 2 tablespoons lemon juice
 1 clove garlic, finely chopped
 1 tablespoon grated onion
 1 tablespoon chopped fresh mint or ¼ teaspoon
   mint extract

Sauté zucchini in oil, turning often until lightly browned. Transfer from pan to glass bowl. Cool. Mix marinade and add to zucchini. Chill at least 1 hour.
Makes 4 servings

Broccoli

 1 bunch fresh broccoli (about 1 pound)
 ¼ cup water

Marinade:

½ cup salad oil
⅓ cup lemon juice
1 clove garlic, finely chopped
Salt and freshly ground pepper to taste

Trim broccoli stems and separate into flowerets. Steam in water until tender but still crisp. Drain. Blend marinade and pour over hot broccoli. Cover and refrigerate until well chilled. Serve cold.
Makes 4 to 6 servings

Spinach-Mushroom Salad with Mustard Marinade

½ pound fresh spinach
1 small head butter lettuce
¼ pound mushrooms, sliced thin
½ green pepper, diced
1 hard-boiled egg

Marinade:

1 tablespoon prepared mustard
1 tablespoon sugar or mild-flavored honey
½ teaspoon salt
¼ teaspoon pepper
¼ cup vinegar
¾ cup oil

Blend mustard, sugar or honey, salt, and pepper. Gradually beat in vinegar until well blended. Beat in oil, then continue beating until the marinade is well blended. Wash, drain, and tear spinach and lettuce into bite-sized pieces. Combine mushrooms and green pepper with ½ of the marinade and chill 1 hour or longer. Combine mixture with greens. Toss. Add more dressing as needed to moisten. Toss again. Garnish with hard-boiled egg slices or wedges.
Makes 4 to 6 sevings

Vinaigrette Vegetables

>2 pints fresh brussels sprouts or two 10-ounce
>   packages frozen brussels sprouts
>1 head cauliflower, separated into flowerets
>1 7-ounce jar artichoke hearts, drained
>8-10 tomato shells (seeds removed)
>Lettuce
>Green pepper rings and sieved hard-cooked eggs
>   for garnish

Marinade:

>1 cup salad oil
>6 tablespoons *each* white wine vinegar and lemon
>   juice
>1½ teaspoons *each* salt and dry mustard
>1 teaspoon sugar

Prepare fresh brussels sprouts by removing stems, cutting into halves, and steaming 10 minutes or until tender or cooking by any other method. Drain. Rinse in cold water and drain again. (Cook frozen vegetables according to package directions.) Prepare and cook cauliflower in a small amount of boiling salted water, about 15 minutes or until crisp-tender. Drain. Rinse with cold water and drain again.

Mix marinade in jar and shake well. Arrange vegetables on a glass tray or in a bowl and pour marinade over vegetables. Cover and refrigerate at least 2 hours, occasionally spooning marinade over vegetables. To serve, remove vegetables with slotted spoon or drain marinade and spoon vegetables into tomato shells on a lettuce leaf for individual salad servings. Garnish with green pepper rings and sieved hard-cooked eggs.
Makes 8 to 10 servings

Mexican Salad

    1 clove garlic, halved
    1 7-ounce can artichoke hearts, quartered
    1 8-ounce can pinto beans, drained
    ½ cucumber, sliced thin
    1 green pepper, cut into ¼-inch-wide strips
    4 radishes, sliced thin
    4 cherry tomatoes, halved
    1 head Bibb lettuce
    4 thin slices chorizo (Mexican pork sausage)
    1 red onion, sliced thin
    4 fresh mushrooms, chopped
    Pinch *each* salt, pepper, and tarragon to taste

Marinade:
    6 tablespoons fresh olive oil
    2 tablespoons wine vinegar
    1 tablespoon *each* lemon juice and salt
    ½ teaspoon coarsely ground black pepper
    1 clove garlic, pressed

Rub salad bowl with cut side of garlic clove. Mix marinade in jar and shake well. Pour ½ of marinade over combined artichoke hearts, beans, cucumber, green pepper, radishes, and tomatoes in a large bowl. Cover and refrigerate overnight. Just before serving, add lettuce, chorizo, onion, mushrooms, salt, pepper, tarragon, and remaining ½ of marinade. Toss lightly. Serve cold.

Variations: For Jewish Salad, substitute chick peas for pinto beans, kosher salami for chorizo. For Italian Salad, substitute garbanzo beans for pinto beans and salami for chorizo.

Makes 6 to 8 servings

Pickled Cabbage

    2 pounds any Chinese cabbage or napa cabbage,
        cut crosswise into 1-inch slices
    1½ cups water
    ½ cup kosher salt or other coarse salt

Combine cabbage, water, and salt in large bowl and let stand at room temperature 1 hour. Drain, pressing out excess liquid.

Marinade-Pickling Solution:
    2½ cups white wine vinegar
    1 tablespoon soft butter
    1 tablespoon pickling spices

Combine cabbage and marinade ingredients in a large bowl, then pack the mixture into 2 1-quart jars. Refrigerate, covered, at least 4 days. Pickled cabbage may be stored, covered tightly, in refrigerator about 3 weeks. For longer storage use canning procedures, which can be found in comprehensive cookbooks under canning/ pickling, or in specialized cookbooks on canning.

Crazy Nell's Pickles

12-15 small cucumbers

Marinade-Pickling Solution:
Fresh dill weed
2 cloves garlic
3-4 small dried red peppers
1 teaspoon salt
1 lump alum or 1 teaspoon powdered alum
1 cup cider vinegar
Cold water

Place cucumbers in 1-quart canning jar that has been warmed and sterilized. Add dill, garlic, peppers, salt, alum, and vinegar. Fill remaining space with cold water. Seal jars. Turn upside down overnight. Turn right side up and store in cool place for 6 weeks.
Makes 10 to 12 servings

Pickled Onions, Hawaiian Style

2 pounds small white Texas or Spanish onions
4 cups water
1 tablespoon table salt

Marinade-Pickling Solution:
4 cups white vinegar
1 cup sugar
1 tablespoon coarse salt
Dash cayenne pepper

Add onions to water and table salt in a bowl, cover, and refrigerate overnight. Drain onions and rinse under cold running water. Heat marinade ingredients in a large saucepan to boiling; simmer 3 minutes. Pack into hot sterilized jars and refrigerate, covered, until cold. May be stored about 3 months.

Makes 10 to 12 servings

Pickled Purple Onions

　　1 large purple onion (about ½ pound), sliced thin

Marinade-Pickling Solution:
　　2 cloves garlic, sliced
　　10 peppercorns
　　¼ teaspoon oregano
　　½ teaspoon salt
　　¾ cup white vinegar (or enough to cover onions in
　　　　1-pint jar)

Place onion in jar with spices and add vinegar to cover. Cover and set in a cool place for 2 to 3 days before using.

Pickled Onion Rings, Mexican Style

Boiling water
2 medium onions, sliced thin and separated into
    rings

Marinade-Pickling Solution:
    ¾ cup white vinegar
    1 teaspoon salt
    ⅛ teaspoon oregano
    1 Mexican dried chile, broken into small pieces, or
        1 cayenne chile, finely sliced
    3 freshly ground peppercorns

Pour boiling water over the onion rings and drain
through a colander. Combine onion rings and mixed
marinade ingredients in a 1-pint jar. Cover and marinate at least 1 hour before using.
Makes 10 to 12 servings

5
Beef Entrées

As food prices escalate, the use of marinades will increase. With marinades, less costly, tougher cuts of meat can be made tender and tantalizing. A blade pot roast, steeped in a peppery marinade for several hours, will have a zippy chile-flavored bite. A standard-grade meat can taste like a choice cut when soaked in an herbed red wine marinade overnight. Or meat from a bony cut can be trimmed away, cubed, and soaked in a tangy spiced solution for skewering and broiling as a kabob.

Marinades must be treated with respect and common sense. When properly used, they enhance flavor and tenderize without being overpowering. It is important to consider the characteristics of the foods and estimate the length of time for marinating.

Beef, lamb, veal, pork, game, poultry, and fish can all be marinated, but their characteristics differ. A thick, tough cut of red meat will take longer to absorb the flavors of the marinade than will a delicate fish or chicken. The recipes in this chapter have all been tested, but they can vary with individual cuts of beef from different parts of the country. So some experimentation is suggested.

It is not necessary to cover completely large cuts of meat or chicken with the marinade. They can be placed in the bowl and turned frequently so all surfaces are eventually immersed in the marinade. Most meats marinate well in 1 or 2 hours at room temperature and 6 hours in the refrigerator. Do not marinate meat longer than 2 hours at room temperature because of potential bacterial growth. The tougher and larger the cut of meat, the longer the marinating time. Very large cuts may require 24 to 48 hours. Roasts and other thick cuts should be pierced to the center with a skewer or knife blade so that the marinade can penetrate and tenderize all the way through.

With each type of entree, basic marinades are offered that you can use with any cooking method you desire— roasting, baking, grilling, and so forth. The same marinades used for steaks and roasts can be used for hamburgers, but hamburgers require only about 30 minutes of marinating at room temperature and 3 hours in the refrigerator.

BASIC STEAK MARINADES

The following basic marinades are suggested for steaks or hamburgers. Prepare ¾ to 1 cup liquid to marinate about 1½ to 2 pounds steak, since the meat does not have to be immersed completely. Steak should be turned once during the minimum marinating time of 2 hours at room temperature or 4 hours in the refrigerator. The same marinades may be used for roasts. Double the amount of liquid for a 3-pound to 5-pound roast. The marinade should reach about two-thirds up the height of the roast, so place roasts in a deep bowl to marinate.

Pierce meat deeply with a skewer in three or four places to allow marinade to penetrate.

After marinating, drain off the liquid and use it for basting and to make sauces and gravies. Broil or grill steaks and hamburgers or bake hamburgers, allowing about 30 minutes at 350° F.

Garlic and Sour Cream on Steak

  2-3 pounds any steak cut

Marinade:
  1 cup dairy sour cream
  1 tablespoon lemon juice
  2 cloves garlic, crushed
  ¼ teaspoon *each* pepper and celery salt
  ½ teaspoon *each* salt and paprika
  1 teaspoon Worcestershire sauce

Combine ingredients and marinate steak, covered, overnight. The same marinade is also delicious when used with chicken.

Makes 4 to 6 servings

Basic Teriyaki Marinade for Meats

2–3 pounds steak or hamburgers

Marinade:
2 tablespoons *each* oil, sugar, and sherry or dry
white wine
1 tablespoon soy sauce
½ cup beef consomme (from canned bouillon or
homemade soup)
1 clove garlic, pressed
4 teaspoons powdered ginger or 1 small (about ⅛
inch) piece fresh ginger root, minced
Salt and pepper to taste

Marinate meat in refrigerator 4 to 6 hours or overnight.
Makes 4 to 6 servings

Basic Sherry Marinade

½ cup dry sherry
¼ cup *each* vegetable oil and olive oil
1 medium onion, finely chopped
1 clove garlic, minced
1 tablespoon chopped fresh parsley
1 teaspoon salt

Mix ingredients and pour over meat. Marinate in refrigerator 2 to 10 hours.
Makes about 1¼ cups

Dieter's Basic Wine Marinade for Steak

¾ cup tarragon vinegar, wine vinegar, or wine
1 medium onion, minced
½ cup chopped parsley
1½ teaspoons garlic, minced

½ teaspoon thyme or cumin
1 bay leaf, crushed
3 drops tabasco sauce or dash red pepper

Combine all ingredients. Marinate 2 to 4 hours.
Makes ¾ cup

Dieter's Broth Marinade for Steak or Lean Hamburger

1 cup instant beef broth
2 tablespoons cider vinegar
2 tablespoons soy sauce
2 cloves garlic, crushed
2 tablespoons parsley
Salt and pepper to taste

Mix all ingredients. Marinate 30 minutes at room temperature or 3 hours in the refrigerator.
Makes 1 cup

Round Steak with Beer Flavor

1 top round steak about 1¼ inches thick

Marinade:
¼ cup packed brown sugar
2 tablespoons prepared German-style mustard
1 tablespoon vinegar
2 teaspoons salt
¼ teaspoon coarsely ground pepper
1 cup beer
1 medium onion, chopped
1 bay leaf

Combine brown sugar, mustard, vinegar, salt, and pepper in saucepan. Heat and slowly stir in beer. Add onion and bay leaf and continue to cook slowly 10 minutes, stirring occasionally. Cool. Place steak in flat dish. Add marinade and turn meat so it is covered with marinade. Cover dish and refrigerate 6 to 8 hours or overnight, turning meat at least once. Drain marinade and barbecue or broil steak. Slice thin.
Makes 4 servings

Italian Round Steak

2-2½ pounds round steak about 1½ inches thick

Marinade:
1 cup prepared Italian dressing
½ cup red wine
1 tablespoon Worcestershire sauce

Combine marinade ingredients and marinate steak 6 hours or overnight. Drain and broil. Slice steak diagonally across grain and serve.
Makes 4 servings

Porterhouse Steak with Zesty Wine Marinade

    1 4-pound porterhouse steak about 1½ inches thick

Marinade:
    ½ cup red burgundy or ⅓ cup bottled steak sauce
    3 tablespoons lemon juice
    2 tablespoons salad oil
    1½ teaspoons sugar
    ½ teaspoon seasoned salt
    ¼ teaspoon pepper

Combine marinade ingredients and pour over steak. Turn meat occasionally during 4-hour marinating period in refrigerator. Drain and broil.
Makes 4 to 6 servings

Flank Steak with Rosé Wine

    1 2-pound flank steak

Marinade:
    ¾ cup rosé wine
    ¼ cup oil
    1 large clove garlic, crushed
    1 teaspoon *each* salt and pepper

Mix marinade, pour over meat, turn meat, and place in refrigerator, covered, 3 to 4 hours. Drain and broil. Cut meat diagonally across the grain into thin slices. Use remaining marinade for sauce.
Makes 3 to 4 servings

Mexican Steak

3 pounds sirloin or porterhouse steak, 2 inches
   thick

Marinade:

2 tablespoons olive oil
¼ cup *each* orange juice and tomato juice
2 tablespoons lime juice
1 teaspoon *each* paprika, cumin seed, and oregano
½ teaspoon red chile pepper
2 teaspoons garlic salt

Mix marinade ingredients and pour over steak. Cover
and refrigerate 6 hours or overnight. Drain and broil
steak.
Makes 6 servings

London Broil, Southern Style

1 London broil or thick-cut flank steak
¼ pound mushrooms, sautéed

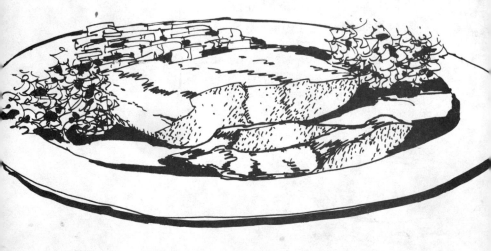

Marinade:

>   1 8-ounce can tomato sauce
>   2 tablespoons bourbon or gin
>   2 tablespoons chopped chives
>   ¼ teaspoon *each* garlic powder, salt, celery salt
>   ½ teaspoon pepper

Combine marinade ingredients and pour over steak and mushrooms. Marinate 3 to 4 hours in refrigerator, turning meat occasionally. Drain, but save marinade. Pat meat dry. Broil. Heat marinade mixture to just under boiling. Slice steak across grain and serve with marinade sauce.

Makes 4 servings

Barbecued Beef, Korean Style

>   1½ pounds boneless beef round, sirloin tip, or
>   chuck steak, cut into individual steak-size
>   servings

Marinade:

>   ⅓ cup *each* oil and soy sauce
>   ¼ cup *each* sugar and minced green onions
>   3 cloves garlic, minced
>   2 tablespoons toasted sesame seeds
>   Dash hot pepper sauce
>   ½ teaspoon salt

Mix marinade and pour over beef. Marinate 4 to 6 hours or overnight in refrigerator. Drain marinade and grill meat. Heat marinade for sauce.

Makes 3 to 4 servings

Steak, Japanese Style

> 1 pound lean sirloin or porterhouse steak, cut into
> thin strips

Marinade:
> ⅓ cup sake or dry sherry
> ⅓ cup soy sauce
> ¼ cup sugar
> 1 teaspoon grated fresh ginger root or ½ teaspoon
> ground ginger
> 1 clove garlic, minced
> ¼ lemon, sliced thin

Add meat slices to combined marinade ingredients. Marinate about 15 minutes and drain. Cook steak slices briefly in hot skillet. The beef tastes best when slightly rare.
Makes 4 servings

Steak Orientale with Italian Dressing

> 2-2½ pounds steak (any favorite cut), about 1-1½
> inches thick
> 1 green pepper, cut into chunks
> 1 onion, sliced

Marinade Orientale:
> 1 cup prepared Italian salad dressing
> ¼ cup soy sauce
> 2 tablespoons brown sugar

Mix marinade and add steak. Cover and marinate in refrigerator 4 hours or overnight, turning occasionally. Broil and brush with liquid. Broil green pepper and onions during last 10 minutes.
Makes 4 to 6 servings

Beef Roast with Orange Flavor

3-4 pounds rump, chuck, eye, or other roast

Marinade:
   ½ cup *each* dry red wine and oil
   ⅓ cup *each* soy sauce and frozen orange juice
      concentrate, thawed
   ¼ teaspoon ground ginger or ¼ teaspoon fresh
      ginger root, grated
   ¼ clove garlic, minced

Pierce roast. Combine marinade ingredients. Pour over roast and marinate in refrigerator overnight. Turn several times while marinating. Drain marinade and roast beef on spit or in oven. Reheat marinade for sauce before serving.
Makes 4 to 6 servings

Prime Rib Roast, Spanish Style

4 pounds rib eye or prime rib roast
1 tablespoon salt

Marinade:
   1 cup wine vinegar
   ½ cup *each* burgundy wine and water
   2 tablespoons gin
   1 tablespoon onion juice
   1 clove garlic, crushed
   1 crushed bay leaf
   ½ teaspoon tarragon
   3 drops hot pepper sauce or 1 small dried hot chile
      pepper, chopped

Mix marinade and pour over meat in a shallow pan. Marinate in refrigerator overnight or at room temperature about 6 hours. Cover. Turn occasionally. If it's been refrigerated, let stand at room temperature about 3 hours before roasting. Remove from marinade; dust with salt. Roast at 300° F. until done to your taste, using a meat thermometer. Baste with marinade every ½ hour.

Makes 4 servings

Seven-Bone Chuck Roast

    5 pounds 7-bone chuck roast
    Unseasoned meat tenderizer

Marinade:
    1 cup catsup
    ½ cup water
    ¼ cup wine vinegar
    2 tablespoons onion soup mix
    2 tablespoons Worcestershire sauce
    1 tablespoon *each* brown sugar and prepared
        mustard
    1 teaspoon chili powder
    ½ teaspoon salt

Sprinkle beef with tenderizer, following label directions. Combine marinade ingredients and heat to boiling. Pour marinade over beef and coat all sides. Marinate at least 1 hour in refrigerator. Drain. Barbecue on spit or roast in oven, basting frequently. Heat marinade and serve as sauce over sliced roast.

Makes 4 servings

Provençal Beef Stew

4 pounds stewing beef, cut into 1½-inch cubes
2 pounds large eggplant
2½ cups chopped onions
¼ cup olive oil
½ pound sliced bacon
1 pint cherry tomatoes or 4 medium tomatoes, chopped
1 10½-ounce can beef bouillon
3 cloves garlic
4 sprigs parsley
2 bay leaves
2 pieces orange rind about ½ inch wide and 3 inches long
4 cloves
¼ cup tomato paste

Marinade:
½ cup *each* cognac and orange juice
3 cups red wine

Mix marinade and combine with beef in large bowl. Marinate 6 hours or longer. Remove meat with slotted spoon and dry on paper towels. Reserve marinade. Dice eggplant and soak in salted water for 30 minutes. Cook onions in oil until tender. Remove onions with slotted spoon and set aside. Preheat oven to 350° F. Brown bacon and set aside. Brown drained eggplant thoroughly and set aside. Cherry tomatoes may be sautéed briefly, then set aside. Brown the beef and combine with the bacon and onion in a 3-quart casserole. Add reserved marinade, beef bouillon, garlic, parsley, bay leaves, orange rind, and cloves. Bake, covered, for 1½ hours or until tender. Stir in tomato paste. Add cherry tomatoes and eggplant and cook 10 minutes longer.
Makes 4 to 6 servings

Courtesy, California Honey Advisory Board

CREATIVITY WITH KABOBS

Kabobs, kebabs, shashlik, shish kebab, spear-its: no matter the name, foods pierced by a stick and cooked over coals are the mainstay of menus in many countries. Somewhere between the hot dog on a stick and the flamboyant flaming sword, there's a universe of delightful dishes loosely termed "skewered foods."

Mixing up tasty treats on sticks requires only a little magic power. Select compatible foods and choose the right marinades to keep them moist and tender while cooking.

Treatment of the meat is essentially the same for all kabobs: the meat is cut into chunks about 1 to 2 inches square and marinated for several hours or overnight in the refrigerator. The meat is laced onto the bamboo or metal skewer by itself or with vegetables and fruits, then barbecued, grilled, or broiled in an oven. The kabob must be turned once or twice while broiling so all sides are cooked. Because many vegetables cook more quickly than the meats, they must be watched carefully and brushed with the marinade frequently during cooking. Vegetables and fruits can be cooked on separate skewers and served with the cooked meat cubes.

The marinades can be interchanged with any of various cuts of meat. Generally 2 cups of liquid marinade will cover about 1 pound of cut-up steak cubes. Remember that marinades tenderize so you can select less costly cuts of beef, trim away all excess fat and bones, cut into cubes, soak, and skewer. Additional kabob recipes for other meats, chicken, and fish will be found in following chapters. Refer to Index.

To assure successful performances, learn the maneuvers of a kabob magician:

- Prevent ingredients from slipping off skewers by

placing a large cube of bread brushed with oil at the pointed end.

- Vegetables that require longer cooking than others, such as onions, potatoes, and zucchini, should be parboiled or placed on separate skewers. Begin to cook them before cooking the meat or chicken.
- Always preheat the broiler and spread oil on the barbecue racks and grills to prevent meat from sticking.
- Keep slippery foods, such as raw oysters or chicken livers, under control by wrapping them in bacon or other meat. Intersperse soft foods with harder foods to give them all a firmer hold.
- Select ingredients for color and texture; combine crunchy things with soft, smooth foods. Complement flavors: sweet and sour, smoky and nutty, zesty and mild.
- Combine fruits and vegetables with meats, chicken, and fish. Almost any food that can be pierced and cooked is a kabob candidate.
- Serve your kabobs with white, brown, or wild rice or with African couscous, or felafel.
- Baste the foods with the marinade during cooking to keep them moist.

BASIC KABOB MARINADES

Each of the following recipes will marinate 1 to 1½ pounds of beef to yield 3 to 4 servings.

Onion Soup Kabob Marinade

    1 envelope onion soup mix
    1 cup salad oil
    ½ cup red wine vinegar
    1 tablespoon soy sauce

Mix ingredients and marinate beef cubes for several hours or refrigerate overnight.

Yogurt Kabob Marinade with Chile Pepper

1½ cups plain yogurt
¾ cup chopped onion
1 teaspoon garlic, minced
½ dried hot chile pepper, chopped
¾ teaspoon cumin seed
½ teaspoon nutmeg
¼ teaspoon *each* salt and cinnamon

Mix all ingredients and toss beef chunks with marinade.
Marinate for several hours or refrigerate overnight.

Mustard Kabob Marinade

¼ cup *each* catsup, vinegar, oil, and water
1 tablespoon prepared mustard
1½ teaspoons salt

Mix all ingredients and pour over beef cubes and marinate for several hours or overnight in the refrigerator.

Spiced Kabob Marinade

⅓ cup soy sauce
¼ cup lemon juice
1 tablespoon brown sugar
2 teaspoons *each* minced garlic, ground caraway
       seeds, and ground coriander seeds
1½ teaspoons salt
¼ teaspoon ground red pepper

Mix all ingredients and toss with meat. Marinate for
several hours or overnight in the refrigerator.

Malaysian Hamburgers

> 1-2 pounds lean ground beef or chopped sirloin
>   shaped as small meat loaves or flattened
>   hamburgers

Marinade:
> 4 fresh mild chiles
> 1 dried hot chile
> 2 small onions
> ½ teaspoon ginger root, chopped
> ¼ cup lemon juice
> 1 tablespoon brown sugar
> Pinch saffron or turmeric
> 1½ cups thick coconut milk
> ¼ teaspoon salt

Crush fresh and dried chiles, onions, and ginger and mix into a paste with lemon juice. Add sugar, saffron or turmeric, salt, and the coconut milk. Pour over meat and let stand, covered, in refrigerator 4 hours, turning meat frequently. Drain. Bake in 350° F. oven ½ hour, or broil or grill. Heat remaining marinade for sauce.
Makes 4 servings

French Hot Dogs

> 8 beef (or pork and beef) hot dogs
> 1 tablespoon flour
> 8 French bread rolls
> 4 tablespoons grated Parmesan cheese

Marinade:
> 1 cup water
> 3 tablespoons lemon juice
> 1 envelope (1-cup serving) *each* dry onion soup mix
>   and dry tomato soup mix
> 1 tablespoon sugar
> ½ teaspoon dry mustard

Score hot dogs diagonally. Mix marinade ingredients and heat together in a frying pan, stirring constantly, until it boils. Remove from heat and add the hot dogs. Let stand, covered, 15 to 20 minutes. Remove the hot dogs from marinade. Broil or grill 4 inches from heat, 7 to 10 minutes, turning frequently. In the meantime, stir flour into the marinade and reheat to boiling, stirring until thick. Serve hot dogs in French rolls. Spoon marinade over hot dogs and sprinkle with Parmesan cheese.
Makes 4 servings

Szechwan Shredded Beef

¾ pound partially frozen flank steak, shredded
3 tablespoons peanut or safflower oil
1 clove garlic, minced
½ tablespoon fresh ginger root, minced
½ cup carrot, shredded
½ fresh hot pepper, shredded
½ cup fresh sweet red pepper, shredded
2 cups snow peas, ends trimmed, strings removed, rinsed, and shredded
4 scallions (white part only), shredded

Marinade:
1 teaspoon light soy sauce
1 tablespoon *each* sherry and water chestnut powder
½ egg white, beaten slightly

Seasoning Sauce:
1 tablespoon *each* hoisin sauce, bean sauce, sherry, Chinese red vinegar, and dark soy sauce
2 teaspoons plum sauce
1 teaspoon hot sauce
1 teaspoon water chestnut powder

Mix marinade and add shredded beef. Cover and refrigerate at least 30 minutes and up to 12 hours.

Mix all seasoning sauce ingredients together in a bowl. Arrange all remaining ingredients except oil on a tray in preparation for stir frying. Heat a wok or electric frying pan to medium heat. Add 1 tablespoon oil and heat 20 seconds until hot but not smoking. Add garlic and ginger and stir fry 15 seconds. Add carrots and stir fry 1 minute. Raise heat to high and add hot and sweet peppers, snow peas, and scallions and fry 1 minute. Transfer all contents of wok with slotted spoon to a heated serving dish.

Add remaining oil to wok and turn heat to high. Stir fry marinated meat in wok until it loses its redness, about 2 minutes. Restir seasoning sauce and add to wok with beef. Return vegetables to wok. Stir fry everything rapidly 1 more minute and mix gently but thoroughly. Transfer to heated serving dish and serve at once.

Note: The recipe may be doubled, but each recipe should be made separately and cooked in successive batches as the wok will not heat all the ingredients sufficiently if too large a quantity is made at one time.

Makes 2 to 3 entrée servings; 4 to 6 servings if other Chinese dishes are served

GREEK GYROS

A popular sandwich is the Greek Gyros made of thin, slivered slices of marinated meat packed into a pocket-type bread or served stacked on a bun. The Gyros can easily be prepared in large quantities for a crowd and barbecued on a spit or in small quantities made on a skewer.

Rather than a large roast, the Gyros meat can be made of assembled slices of a beef, lamb, or pork roast. The marinade penetrates the meat when the slices are marinated and then combined. You can buy a boneless roast, but it is less costly and equally as efficient to buy a roast with a bone, then bone it yourself and assemble the meat. Use the bone for soups. Use a beef cross-rib roast, a leg of lamb, or a pork loin or leg (ham shank). Soak the steaks overnight in the marinade, then reassemble, as shown, and barbecue on a rotisserie.

Gyros Roast, Greek Style

3 pounds boneless roast, cut into ½-inch-thick steak slices

Marinade:
¼ cup *each* olive oil and dry white wine
3 tablespoons lime or lemon juice
¼ teaspoon *each* oregano leaves, crushed bay leaf, freshly ground black pepper
2 cloves garlic, minced
2 tablespoons finely chopped fresh parsley

Slice beef and soak in marinade, covered, overnight in refrigerator. Reassemble, as shown in the drawings on pages 82–83.
Makes 12 to 15 servings

Greek Cucumber-Tomato Salad

6 large tomatoes, peeled and seeded
2 large cucumbers, peeled and seeded

Marinade:
½ cup olive or salad oil
¼ cup white wine vinegar
1 teaspoon *each* oregano and pepper
2 teaspoons finely chopped fresh parsley

Cut vegetables into ½-inch cubes. Mix marinade. Pour over vegetables and refrigerate, covered, overnight and until ready to serve.

1. Remove steaks from marinade and stack and shape slices so they assume the shape of the original roast, and are wide enough to span the barbecue spit forks.

2. Tie the meat slices securely with string. Insert the spit through the center and secure with the forks on each side. Insert meat thermometer. Cook over coals about 1½ to 2 hours or until meat thermometer registers the proper temperature for the type of meat you are using. Lift spit onto a platter and let meat stand 10 minutes before carving.

3. *To carve,* remove one spit fork and push the roast to the end of the spit. Cut off strings and cut meat, as shown, so it falls into narrow strips. Pile into pocket bread or onto buns. It may be topped with Greek Cucumber-Tomato Salad and a dollop of plain or lime yogurt.

MARINATED BEEF JERKY

Marinated dried meats make easily stored high-protein snacks and appetizers. They will keep almost indefinitely at room temperature. They can be taken on camp-outs and hikes. If you partially freeze the meat before preparation, it will be easier to slice in the narrow strips required, or have your butcher slice it for you. Cut meat *across* the grain for a tender, slightly brittle jerky. Cut *with* the grain if you like it chewier.

Spicy Mexican Jerky

> 1-1½ pounds boneless beef top round steak, flank steak, chuck, or other "special" roast buy of the week

Marinade:
> 2 tablespoons *each* water and Worcestershire sauce
> 1 teaspoon *each* salt and cumin
> 2 cloves garlic, pressed
> 1½ teaspoons chili powder
> ⅛ teaspoon cayenne

Trim all fat from meat and discard. Slice meat ⅛ inch thick and make the slices as long as possible, either with or across the grain, as indicated above.

Combine marinade ingredients in a bowl, stir well, and add meat slices. Mix thoroughly and refrigerate overnight. Drain meat. Shake off excess liquid and discard marinade. Arrange strips of meat close together but not overlapping on a broiler rack set in a foil-lined, rimmed baking or broiling pan to catch drips.

Bake uncovered in 200° F. oven about 5 to 6 hours or until meat feels dry and is a dark brown. Pat off any remaining oil with a paper towel. Cool. Remove from racks and store in airtight containers.

Makes about 6 ounces

Herb-Wine Jerky

> 1–1½ pounds boneless beef top round steak, flank steak, chuck, or other "special" roast buy of the week

Marinade:

> ¾ cup burgundy wine
> 2 cloves garlic, pressed
> 1 tablespoon thyme leaves
> 2 bay leaves
> 1 teaspoon *each* salt and Worcestershire sauce
> ¼ teaspoon pepper

Trim all fat from meat and discard. Slice meat ⅛ inch thick and make the slices as long as possible, either with or across the grain.

Mix marinade ingredients and simmer for 5 minutes. Transfer to a large bowl and cool. Add the meat. Marinate, then bake as for Spicy Mexican Jerky.

Hawaiian Jerky (Pipi Kaula)

   1–1½ pounds boneless beef top round steak, flank
      steak, chuck, or other "special" roast buy of
      the week.

Marinade:
   ¼ cup soy sauce
   ¼ cup dry sherry
   1 small onion, minced
   2 tablespoons minced ginger
   1 clove garlic, minced
   1½ teaspoons coarse salt

Trim all fat from meat and discard. Cut into ½-inch-thick 4″ × 1″ strips and pound with a mallet to tenderize.

Combine marinade ingredients in a bowl, stir well, and add meat slices. Mix thoroughly and refrigerate overnight. Drain meat. Shake off excess liquid and discard marinade. Arrange strips of meat close together but not overlapping on a broiler rack set in a foil-lined, rimmed baking or broiling pan to catch drips.

Bake uncovered in 200° F. oven about 5 to 6 hours or until meat feels dry and is a dark brown. Pat off any remaining oil with a paper towel. Cool. Remove from racks and store in airtight containers.

Jerky may be broiled or pan fried until hot, 5 to 8 minutes, and served with green onions and salt.

6
Lamb, Veal, and Pork Entrées

Herbs and spices, wines, flavored liqueurs, mustards, and fruit-flavored jellies and jams are the sparkling, taste appealing ingredients used in the marinades for lamb, veal, and pork in the recipes from various countries. They provide an extra piquancy, a subtle difference that makes the meal memorable. As you read and compare the recipes and experiment with the ingredients, observe the minor differences in the recipes from one country to another—just enough to give them a unique cultural characteristic. Such recipes are easy to emulate and fun to prepare because of the delicious results.

In South Africa lamb is the basis of many kabob recipes called sosaties. In Russia the skewered foods are dubbed shashlik and in Persia chelo kebab. Some cultures use a sweet-sour sauce, others herbs and spices and sometimes yogurt. Often entire legs of lamb are marinated and roasted on spits over the coals.

Veal is the meat of a young cow and the animal is usually carefully fed so the meat is very tender. Choice veal is delicate and tasty without additives, but some veal chops and shoulder cuts can be given interesting flavors with different marinades, and a Mexican version is offered here.

Marinades also kill the wild taste of game, such as venison. There are entire books dealing with the taste-taming of game and the hunter is advised to consult such volumes for these foods.

Pork, available in a wide variety of cuts, is a perfect food for marinating; and recipes begin on page 100. Whether your favorite cuts are pork chops, shoulder, or spareribs, the choice of marinades will allow you to experiment until you find the combinations for the flavors you prefer.

Recipes for lamb, veal, and pork may be oven-baked, broiled, or grilled outdoors. When you decide on a basic marinade, select the method of cooking from one of the other recipes suggesting heat and time. Allow about ½ cup of marinade for each pound of lamb, veal, or pork.

BASIC MARINADES FOR LAMB

Marinating time is 1 to 2 hours at room temperature or 3 to 4 hours in the refrigerator.

Mint Marinade

    ½ cup water
    1 tablespoon cider vinegar
    1 cup orange or clover honey
    ⅓ cup minced fresh mint or ¼ cup dried mint flakes

Bring water and vinegar to a boil. Add honey and stir until dissolved. Remove from heat and stir in mint. Use to marinate any lamb cuts for broiling or barbecuing.
Makes about 1¾ cups to marinate 3 to 4 pounds meat

Armenian Herb Marinade

> ½ cup olive oil or salad oil
> ½ cup tomato juice
> ½ cup finely chopped onion
> ¼ cup lemon juice
> ¼ cup snipped parsley
> 1 clove garlic, minced
> 1 teaspoon *each* salt, dried marjoram, and dried
>   thyme, crushed
> ½ teaspoon pepper

Combine all ingredients and pour marinade mixture over lamb cuts to be broiled or barbecued, in covered dish. Marinate in refrigerator 6 hours or overnight. Be sure to turn meat in marinade so all sides are coated. (This recipe may also be used for pork and chicken.)
Makes 1¾ cups to marinate 3 to 4 pounds of meat

Dieter's Spice Marinade

> 1 cup wine vinegar
> 1 onion, chopped
> 8 whole cloves
> 2 sprigs fresh mint or 1 teaspoon chopped dried
>   mint
> 2 cloves garlic, crushed
> 4 sprigs fresh parsley or 1 teaspoon dried parsley
> ⅛ teaspoon *each* thyme and tarragon
> 1 teaspoon grated lemon rind
> 2 teaspoons salt

Mix all ingredients and pour over lamb.
Makes 1 cup for 1 or 2 servings of lamb chops or other lamb cuts

Lamb Chops L'Orange

6 shoulder lamb chops, ¾ inch thick
2 oranges, cut into 6 wedges each
1 to 2 tablespoons cornstarch

Marinade:

½ cup orange juice or ¼ cup frozen orange juice
concentrate, thawed
3 tablespoons soy sauce
2 teaspoons sugar
1 teaspoon garlic salt
1 teaspoon ground ginger
⅛ teaspoon pepper

Arrange chops in flat glass baking dish. Combine marinade ingredients, pour over chops, cover, and refrigerate 2 hours. Cover and bake with marinade at 350° F., 1 hour or until tender. Transfer chops to serving plate and garnish with orange wedges. Skim fat from drippings; thicken drippings with 1 tablespoon cornstarch per cup of juice. Spoon over meat and oranges.
Makes 6 servings

Portuguese-Style Lamb Chops

6 shoulder lamb chops, ¾ inch thick

Marinade:

½ cup oil
4 tablespoons rose wine
1 small onion, sliced
1 clove garlic, chopped
1 tablespoon Dijon-style mustard
1 teaspoon salt
⅛ teaspoon pepper

Mix marinade ingredients and pour over chops arranged in flat baking dish, covering both sides evenly. Cover and refrigerate 8 hours. Drain the marinade. Oven broil or charcoal broil until tender. Chops may be baked uncovered in 350° F. oven 50 to 60 minutes. Baste often with added marinade if liquid cooks off.
Makes 6 servings

Dinner Party Lamb Roast

> 6 pounds boneless lamb shoulder
> ¼ cup shortening
> Lemon-Spice Gravy (see recipe)
> 6 tablespoons all-purpose flour

Marinade:
> 2½ cups canned condensed beef broth or bouillon
> 2 tablespoons mixed pickling spices
> 1½ teaspoons poultry seasoning
> 3 tablespoons grated lemon peel
> 3 tablespoons lemon juice

Place roast in a deep glass bowl. Mix marinade ingredients and heat just to boiling. Pour over lamb and refrigerate until marinade cools. Turn meat to coat thoroughly. Cover tightly and refrigerate 24 hours, turning meat frequently.

Remove meat from marinade and brown in shortening over medium heat, about 15 minutes. Pour off fat. Strain marinade and pour 1 cup over lamb. Reserve the remaining marinade for sauce. Bake lamb in covered pan in 325° F. oven 2½ to 3 hours or until done. Serve with Lemon-Spice Gravy recipe (page 94).
Makes 10 to 12 servings

Lemon-Spice Gravy

Pour fat and juices from pan into bowl, but leave the brown particles in the pan. Allow fat to rise to top and skim off, but reserve ¼ cup. Place reserved fat in saucepan. Gradually blend in flour. Cook over low heat, stirring as mixture thickens and bubbles. Remove from heat. Measure remaining marinade; add water to yield 3 cups liquid; stir into flour mixture. Heat to boiling, stirring constantly. Boil and stir 1 minute. Pour over roast lamb just before serving.
Makes 12 servings

Minted Leg of Lamb

   1 3-4 pound leg of lamb, boned and butterflied

Marinade:
   ½ cup oil
   1 cup white wine or dry vermouth
   2 garlic cloves, crushed
   1 teaspoon dried mint flakes, crushed, or 3 fresh
      mint leaves
   ½ teaspoon dried orange peel or freshly scraped
      peel
   ½ teaspoon salt
   ¼ teaspoon pepper

Have butcher bone and butterfly lamb so it can be laid out flat for broiling. Marinate lamb in mixture and place in a covered dish in refrigerator overnight. Turn several times. Drain. Oven broil or charcoal broil until browned on both sides and meat thermometer in thickest part registers about 140° to 150° F.
Makes 6 to 8 servings

Stuffed Leg of Lamb

    1 leg of lamb, boned
    ½ teaspoon salt
    1 can frozen pineapple-grapefruit juice
        concentrate, mixed with 1½ cups water
    2 grated apples
    ½ cup bread crumbs
    ½ teaspoon crushed rosemary
    1 teaspoon crushed mint
    2 tablespoons butter

Marinade:
    1 cup white wine
    ½ of above fruit juice mixture
    1 tablespoon salad oil

Spread lamb and salt interior. Combine ½ of juice with apples, crumbs, rosemary, mint, and butter and spread over inside of meat. Roll lamb back into original leg shape and tie with twine.

Mix marinade ingredients and pour over meat in roasting pan. Cover and refrigerate overnight, turning occasionally. Drain. Place meat on a rack in a roasting pan and roast at 450° F. for 15 minutes; then reduce heat and bake at 325° F. about 2 hours or until tender. Baste frequently with marinade. Skim off fat and thicken pan juices as for Lemon-Spice Gravy recipe (page 94).
Makes 6 to 8 servings

LAMB KABOBS

Follow the same directions as for Beef Kabobs (Chapter 5). Serve with white rice or saffron rice.

Indonesian Sate Lamb Kabobs

1½ pounds lamb shoulder or leg, cut into 1-inch cubes
½ cup tomato sauce
¼ cup beef stock or water
1 teaspoon tabasco sauce

Marinade:

½ cup soy sauce mixed with 1 teaspoon dark molasses
¾ cup hot water
⅓ cup chunky-style peanut butter
½ cup peanuts without skins, toasted in oven, chopped or ground
1 teaspoon red pepper flakes
1 garlic clove, minced
2 tablespoons lemon juice

Mix marinade ingredients in saucepan. Bring to boil and stir until fairly smooth. Let cool. Pour ½ the sauce over lamb cubes and marinate at least 2 hours. Add tomato sauce, stock or water, and tabasco to other half of marinade. Remove lamb cubes from marinade and add remaining marinade to sauce. Bring to boil and stir. Use for basting and as a dipping sauce when serving. Place marinated cubes on small wooden skewers and broil. *Makes 4 to 6 servings*

Lamb Kabob with Beer-Pineapple Marinade

1½ pounds lamb shoulder or leg, cut into 1½-inch cubes
1 large green pepper
2 large tomatoes

2 small onions
8 2-inch cubes fresh pineapple

Marinade:

½ cup beer
½ cup juice from fresh pineapple
2 tablespoons oil
1 tablespoon soy sauce
1 clove garlic, crushed

Mix marinade ingredients. Add lamb and refrigerate, covered, overnight. Seed and cut pepper into 2-inch cubes; quarter tomatoes; peel and quarter onions. Drain marinade. Alternate lamb, vegetables, and pineapples on skewers. Brush on marinade while broiling.
Makes 4 servings

Lamb-Ham Kabob

1 pound lamb shoulder or leg, cut into 1½-inch
    cubes
½ pound cooked ham, cut into 1-inch cubes
1 small apple, cut into 8 wedges
1 8-ounce can pineapple chunks in heavy syrup

Marinade:

Pineapple syrup drained from 8-ounce can
1 10½-ounce can mushroom gravy
1 tablespoon soy sauce
1 teaspoon curry powder
1 clove garlic, minced
Dash ground ginger

Drain pineapple and combine juice with other marinade ingredients. Add lamb and ham. Marinate 6 hours or overnight, covered, in refrigerator. Drain. Arrange ham and lamb alternately on 2 skewers. On separate skewers, arrange pineapple chunks and apple slices. Broil meat skewers on coals or in oven 5 minutes, turning and brushing with sauce. Place fruit kabobs over heat and cook 10 minutes more or until lamb is done.
Makes 4 servings

VEAL

Mexican-Style Barbecued Veal Chops

6 veal chops, 1½ inches thick, rinsed and dried

Marinade:
½ cup cider vinegar
¼ cup *each* vegetable oil and catsup
½ cup minced onion
1 clove garlic, minced
½ teaspoon *each* crumbled thyme leaves, ground
    cumin, chili powder
¼ teaspoon ground red pepper
1½ teaspoons salt

Combine marinade ingredients and add chops. Marinate in refrigerator 6 hours. Drain chops and broil 5 inches from heat 15 to 20 minutes or until brown. Baste with marinade.
Makes 6 servings

Basic Lemon Marinade for Veal

¾ cup wine vinegar
3 tablespoons lemon juice
1 medium onion, minced
1 clove garlic, crushed
1 bay leaf, crumbled
¼ cup chopped parsley
⅛ teaspoon *each* thyme and tarragon
2 teaspoons salt
½ teaspoon pepper

Marinate veal in refrigerator a minimum of 4 hours.
Makes about 1 cup of marinade for 2 pounds of veal

Venison Sauerbraten

5-6 pounds leg of venison, skinned, boned, and tied
for roasting
⅓ cup cooking oil

Marinade:

3 cups dry white wine
1¼ cups olive oil
2 *each* sliced onions, sliced carrots, and mashed
garlic cloves
1 teaspoon salt
1 bay leaf
2 tablespoons chopped parsley
¼ teaspoon thyme
8 peppercorns
1 clove
6 coriander seeds
6 juniper berries, crushed, or ¼ cup red currant
jelly

Sauce:

3 tablespoons all-purpose flour
3 tablespoons softened butter
½ cup ginger liqueur or brandy
Salt and pepper to taste

Mix marinade ingredients and pour over venison in a
stainless steel or glass dish. Marinate 48 hours, turning
leg several times. Remove venison from marinade and
reserve marinade. Dry venison and rub with cooking
oil. Place in shallow pan and roast in 450° F. oven 30 to
40 minutes or until well browned. Move venison to
large stewing pot. Add marinade, bring to a boil, and
skim. Reduce flame. Make a smooth paste of flour and
butter and stir into pot. Simmer, covered, until venison
is very tender, about 1 hour. Add liqueur, salt and

pepper to taste, and parsley. Transfer meat from pot to a serving platter. Strain sauce and serve in a gravy boat. *Makes 10 to 12 servings*

PORK

Many pork cuts can have a delicious flavor and aroma when marinated for 2 to 3 hours before roasting, barbecuing, or broiling.

If you cook pork frequently, you may wish to prepare a special spice mix to add to other marinade ingredients. The spice mix can be used with any combination of acid and oil in place of, or in addition to, those suggested in the following basic recipes. The spice mix may be used for pork roasts, pork chops, barbecued ribs, ham slices, and patés, whether or not you are marinating them.

Special Spice Seasoning Mix for Pork

> 2 tablespoons *each* ground bay leaves, cloves, mace, nutmeg, paprika, and thyme
> 2 tablespoons *each* ground dried basil, cinnamon, and savory or parsley
> 5 tablespoons ground white pepper

For any spices not already ground or crushed, you can use a spice grinder or electric blender. Mix ingredients and store in an airtight jar on the spice shelf.

BASIC PROCEDURES FOR SPARERIBS

The following basic marinades are delicious for barbecued spareribs. Each will marinate about 4 pounds of lean pork ribs. For a final glaze, mix a little mustard with honey and brush on ribs.

Strip membrane from back of ribs. Select any of the following marinades. If the ribs are fatty, drop them in boiling water for about 5 minutes before marinating. Remove from water and wipe dry with paper toweling. Place ribs in shallow pan. Combine marinade ingredients and pour over ribs. Cover and marinate at least 2 hours in refrigerator or overnight, turning so both sides soak in the liquid. Drain and reserve marinade and use for basting.

To roast: Place ribs on racks in shallow pans and roast at 350° F. 1¼ hours.

To barbecue: Place on grill, bone side down, 3 inches from low heat. Barbecue about 1¼ hours, turning every 15 minutes.

Makes 4 servings

Curried Marinade for Spareribs

¼ cup soy sauce
3 tablespoons lemon juice
2 tablespoons sherry
1 teaspoon curry powder
1½ cups water with 1½ teaspoons instant tea
    dissolved in it or 1½ cups very strong tea
2 garlic cloves, minced
1 tablespoon Special Spice Seasoning Mix for Pork
    (see recipe)
¼ teaspoon hot pepper sauce

Combine all ingredients. Pour over ribs and marinate overnight.

Mustard Marinade for Spareribs

½ cup *each* cider vinegar, chili sauce, catsup
2 tablespoons lemon juice
1 tablespoon Worcestershire sauce
3 tablespoons brown sugar
2 teaspoons dry mustard
1 garlic clove, finely chopped
½ cup green onion, chopped
1 teaspoon Special Spice Seasoning Mix for Pork
    (see recipe)
1 teaspoon salt
½ teaspoon pepper

Mix ingredients and marinate spareribs 2 to 3 hours.
Makes about 2 cups marinade for 4 to 6 pounds ribs

Teriyaki Sauce for Spareribs

½ cup soy sauce
¼ cup dry wine
2 tablespoons wine vinegar
2 tablespoons honey
2 teaspoons ground ginger
1 large clove garlic, crushed
1 teaspoon Special Spice Seasoning Mix for Pork
    (see recipe)

Mix ingredients and marinate ribs 2 hours or longer.
Makes about 1 cup marinade for 2 to 3 pounds ribs

Cooked Marinade for Pork

The following marinade may be used for any pork cuts.
It is also tasty with game, beef, and lamb.

3 cups water
1 cup red wine vinegar
2 onions, chopped
1 carrot, chopped
2 celery stalks, chopped
3 tablespoons parsley
2 tablespoons Special Spice Seasoning Mix for Pork
(see recipe)

Place all ingredients in a pot and bring to a boil. Simmer for 1 hour. Cool thoroughly. Marinate pork in mixture for at least 3 hours. Do not use marinade for basting.
Makes about 3 cups for approximately 5 to 6 pounds of meat

Dry Marinade for Pork

This marinade can be used for all pork cuts.

2 garlic cloves, peeled
2 teaspoons salt
2 tablespoons Special Spice Seasoning Mix for Pork
(see recipe)
2 tablespoons grated lemon or orange rind

Crush the garlic with the salt until the mixture is like a purée and all the salt has absorbed the garlic oil. Add the other ingredients and mash together. Pierce the meat in several places with a fork or skewer and rub the marinade where the holes are. Rub the remaining marinade over the surface of the meat. Place in covered dish in refrigerator and marinate about 6 hours. Prepare pork by any baking, broiling, or frying method.

Pork Blade Steaks in Beer

4-6 pork blade steaks cut ½ to ¾ inches thick

Marinade:
   1 cup *each* beer and bottled barbecue sauce
   ½ cup chopped onion
   1 teaspoon Special Spice Seasoning Mix for Pork
      (see recipe)
   ⅛ teaspoon garlic powder

Marinate steaks in mixture, covered, in refrigerator about 4 hours, turning steaks several times. Remove steaks from marinade and grill at moderate temperature 20 minutes on 1 side. Brush with marinade and grill on other side until done, about 10 minutes on second side for ½-inch steak and about 15 minutes for ¾-inch steak. *Makes 4 to 6 servings*

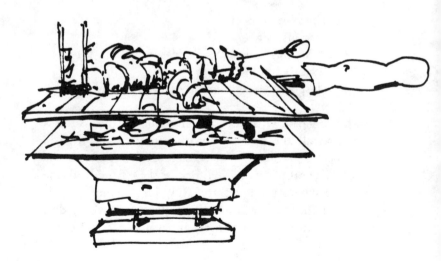

Barbecued Ham Steaks

> 6 1-inch-thick ham steaks

Marinade:
> 4 cups sherry
> ½ cup melted butter
> 4 teaspoons *each* ground cloves and paprika
> ½ cup brown sugar
> ½ teaspoon dry mustard
> 8 garlic cloves, finely chopped

Combine marinade ingredients and marinate ham steaks in mixture for 3 hours, turning once. Oven broil or barbecue; turn frequently and baste with marinade.
Makes 6 servings

7
Poultry Entrées

Chicken is a mainstay of our diets. How many ways do you prepare it? A few basic recipes that you are tired of fixing? If so, it is time to change those menus from the ordinary to something extra special—like taking a basic black dress and giving it a new look with a beautiful scarf or jewels.

A new taste is in store for the marinade-conscious cook. And chicken is infinite in its variety. Study the recipes, pull the ingredients off your shelves, and stir up a marinade that will seem like a delicious elixir. Then watch your diners lick their chicken bones and ask for more.

Chicken breasts soaked in a soy sauce marinade become a teriyaki chicken that would do any exotic Oriental cook proud. Add an orange flavor and, voilà! You are a French chef extraordinaire! With a little pineapple and lemon juice, you can almost imagine a grass-skirted hula dancer. That's how easy it is to change the aura of chicken with marinades.

Prepare your marinated chickens any way you like:

roast them covered, then brown uncovered the last 15 minutes; bake them uncovered and baste frequently; or broil, fry, or cook in a pot.

You will also notice that many of the recipes in this chapter are designed to add color to the chicken to make it attractive and appetizing. Use prepared French and Italian dressings to make it even easier. There is a whole world of ethnic recipes, too, and you will find several in this chapter.

Marinate a whole chicken or parts. Chicken should be well thawed and patted dry. Pierce parts with a fork so the marinade flavors can penetrate the meat and tenderize it. Figure approximately ½ cup marinade per pound of chicken or ¾ cup to 1 cup for a small chicken or the equivalent of 2 chicken breasts. Marinate chicken in glass or ceramic baking dishes in 1 or 2 layers and turn the chicken parts so the skin side is down once or twice during the marinating time, usually a minimum of 2 hours. Some recipes call for baking the chicken in the marinade; for others, you pour off the liquid and use it for basting and thickening for a delectable sauce.

BASIC CHICKEN MARINADES

Lime-Flavored Marinade

   3 tablespoons salad oil
   ½ cup lime juice
   1 tablespoon grated lime peel
   ¼ teaspoon *each* salt and pepper
Makes about ⅔ cup for 1 chicken

Green Onion and Soy Sauce Marinade

   ½ cup soy sauce
   ½ cup thinly sliced green onions
   2 tablespoons dry sherry

2 tablespoons brown sugar
½ teaspoon *each* salt and ground ginger
Makes 1 cup for 1 chicken

Chili Sauce Marinade

1 cup chili sauce
¼ cup red wine vinegar
½ tablespoon horseradish
1 clove garlic, minced
½ teaspoon seasoned salt
Makes 1½ cups for 1 to 2 chickens

Polynesian Marinade

¼ cup honey
¼ cup fresh orange juice
2 tablespoons fresh lemon juice
¼ cup soy sauce
6 kumquats, finely chopped
2 tablespoons grated orange peel
½ teaspoon ground ginger
¼ teaspoon pepper

Blend well in blender.
Makes 1½ cups for 1 to 2 chickens

Italian Tarragon Marinade

½ cup olive oil
¼ cup vinegar, or dry vermouth or white wine
1 teaspoon *each* dried tarragon and parsley
½ teaspoon *each* crumbled dried thyme and celery
seeds

Note: For a lower calorie marinade, substitute instant chicken broth for olive oil.
Makes ¾ cup for 1 chicken

Dieter's Basic Lemon Recipe for Chicken

¾ cup wine vinegar
3 tablespoons lemon juice
1 medium onion, minced
1 clove garlic, crushed
¼ cup chopped parsley
1 bay leaf
⅛ teaspoon *each* thyme and tarragon
2 teaspoons salt
½ teaspoon pepper

Mix marinade and pour over food. Let stand, covered, at least 2 hours in refrigerator.
Makes ¾ cup for 1 chicken

Dry Marinade

A dry marinade has a minimum amount of liquid; it is brushed on the poultry rather than poured over it, covered, and refrigerated overnight.

1 tablespoon salad oil
2 tablespoons brandy, lemon juice, or lime juice
1 clove garlic, crushed
1 teaspoon salt
½ teaspoon *each* crushed cumin seed and dried
    tarragon or basil
Makes marinade for 1 chicken or parts for 2 servings

Cindy's Jam-Boree Baked Chicken

Serve your chicken with marinades that make them colorful as well as tasty.

1-2 chickens, cut up

Marinade I—Red:
   1 8-ounce bottle prepared red salad dressing
        (Russian, Catalina, etc.)
   ½-cup jar red or purple preserves or jelly (any
        flavor, any kind—strawberry, grape, plum, or
        a combination, *or* use ¼ cup jalapeno jelly)
   1 envelope dry onion soup mix

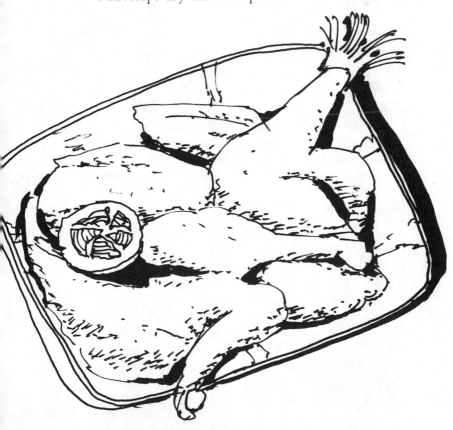

Mix marinade ingredients in small bowl. Lay chicken pieces in flat pan in a single layer and spread with marinade. Cover and refrigerate 3 hours. Bake with marinade at 350° F. 45 minutes to 1 hour.

Marinade II—Green:
>1 bottle green salad dressing (Green Goddess)
>½ cup light-colored preserves or jam (apricot, pineapple, peach, etc.)
>1 package dry onion soup mix

Follow directions for Marinade I.
Makes 4 to 6 servings

Oriental Spiced Chicken

>3-4 whole chicken breasts, split and boned, or 8 chicken legs with thighs attached

Marinade:
>1 cup light soy sauce
>1 cup dry white wine or sherry
>2 cloves garlic, minced
>2 teaspoons pared ginger root, minced

Sauce:
>1 cup dry white wine or sherry
>½ cup hoisin sauce
>½ cup catsup
>¼ cup packed dark brown sugar
>1 clove garlic, minced

Mix marinade and pour over chicken. Refrigerate, covered, at least 4 hours or overnight, turning chicken occasionally. Drain marinade and discard. Arrange chicken, skin side down, in baking dish. Combine sauce ingredients and pour ½ over chicken. Bake at 350° F.

for 25 minutes, then turn chicken skin side up. Add remainder of sauce and bake another 25 minutes or until tender, basting occasionally.
Serve with sauce.
Makes 6 servings

Baked Honey Chicken

> 2 frying chickens, halved or cut up
> Cold water
> 1 tablespoon cornstarch
> Hot cooked rice

Marinade:

> ¼ cup soy sauce
> ½ cup catsup
> ¼ cup fresh lemon juice
> ¼ cup honey or brown sugar

Pour marinade over chicken, which has been arranged in a single layer in a flat dish. Refrigerate several hours or overnight. Cover with foil and bake 1 hour at 325° F. Remove foil, baste with sauce, and bake uncovered 10 to 15 minutes until tender and browned. To thicken sauce, mix a little cold water with 1 tablespoon cornstarch, then stir into sauce. Serve over hot cooked rice.
Makes 4 to 6 servings

Baked Teriyaki-Whiskey Chicken

> 1 large frying chicken

Marinade:

> ⅔ cup *each* salad oil, soy sauce, and bourbon
> 1 teaspoon garlic salt
> ½ teaspoon pepper

Cut chicken into serving pieces, place in a single layer in a pan, and place marinade mixture over surface. Refrigerate 4 hours or overnight. Bake in marinade, covered, in 350° F. oven for 45 minutes or until chicken is well done. Turn pieces frequently and baste with sauce. Cover and bake until brown, about 10 minutes.
Makes 4 servings

Apple-Flavored Chicken Kabobs

>4 chicken breasts, split
>Salt and pepper to taste
>8 mushrooms
>8 small white onions
>8 cherry tomatoes
>2 oranges, quartered
>2 pineapple slices, quartered

Marinade:
>¼ cup oil
>1 cup dry red wine
>2 tablespoons vinegar
>2 tablespoons soy sauce
>1 6-ounce can frozen concentrated apple juice, thawed
>Dash of ginger

Bone chicken breasts and cut each half-breast into 4 pieces. Sprinkle chicken with salt and pepper. Alternate chicken pieces with mushrooms, onions, cherry tomatoes, orange quarters, and pineapple quarters to make 8 skewers. Place skewers in a shallow pan. Combine marinade ingredients and spoon over kabobs. Let stand 1 hour. Drain and broil or barbecue 6 inches from heat, 15 minutes on each side. Brush with marinade every 5 minutes.
Makes 8 servings

California Barbecued Chicken

> 2–3 pounds frying chicken, cut into pieces or
> quartered

Marinade:
> ½ cup sherry
> ⅓ cup honey
> 2 tablespoons lime juice
> 2 teaspoons cinnamon
> ½ teaspoon *each* curry powder and garlic salt

Combine marinade ingredients and pour over chicken. Cover and refrigerate 4 hours. Broil or barbecue 6 inches from heat until tender. Baste often with remaining marinade. Chicken will brown quickly, so watch it closely.

Makes 4 servings

Persian Chicken Kabobs

> 4 chicken breasts, halved, skinned, and boned, cut
> into 2-inch pieces
> 2 teaspoons salt
> 4 medium tomatoes, quartered
> 16 small white onions, peeled
> 2 green peppers, seeded and cut into skewer pieces
> 16 small to medium mushroom caps
> Rice pilaf or plain cooked rice

Marinade:

    ¼ cup *each* corn oil and tarragon wine vinegar
    ½ teaspoon dried mint leaves
    ¼ teaspoon rosemary
    1 clove garlic, crushed
    ¼ teaspoon hot pepper sauce

Sprinkle chicken with 1 teaspoon salt. Mix marinade and pour over chicken in flat dish. Refrigerate at least 2 hours or overnight, turning once or twice, Drain and reserve liquid for basting.

    Thread chicken pieces on skewers, alternating with tomatoes, onions, green peppers, and mushroom caps. Brush with marinade. Sprinkle with remaining 1 teaspoon salt. Broil or cook 30 minutes on outdoor grill about 6 inches from heat or until chicken is done. Turn and baste while cooking. Serve with rice pilaf or plain cooked rice.

Makes 6 servings

Tandoori Chicken Breasts

    4 chicken breasts, quartered
    ¼ cup margarine, melted

Marinade:

    1 cup plain yogurt
    Juice of 1 lime
    2 green chile peppers, cut up
    2 cloves garlic, minced
    1 teaspoon fresh ginger, minced
    1½ teaspoons ground coriander
    1 teaspoon ground cumin
    ½ teaspoon cayenne pepper

Skin chicken breasts and slash chicken diagonally with shallow cuts. Blend ½ the yogurt with remaining ingre-

dients. When well blended, add to the rest of the yogurt and stir to blend. Brush onto cut side of chicken and marinate 8 hours or overnight. Remove chicken from marinade and broil or barbecue 30 to 40 minutes. Coat with melted margarine before cooking. Brush with marinade while cooking and turn once.
Makes 6 to 8 servings

Ecuadorian Chicken-in-a-Pot

    1 3-pound chicken, cut up
    1½ cups flour
    1½ teaspoon *each* salt and pepper
    2 tablespoons shortening or salad oil
    1 large onion, chopped
    1 clove garlic, minced
    4 medium tomatoes, peeled and chopped
    1 bay leaf
    ½ teaspoon *each* oregano, thyme, and crushed dried
        chiles
    2 carrots, chopped
    2 large potatoes, peeled and quartered
    1 cup stuffed green olives
    12 prunes, pitted
    3 green bananas, peeled and cut into 1-inch pieces
    3 tablespoons sugar
    Cooked rice
    Avocado slices for garnish (optional)

Marinade:
>   2 cups dry white wine

Marinate chicken in wine overnight. Drain chicken thoroughly, reserving marinade. Dredge chicken in flour seasoned with salt and pepper. Heat shortening in a large kettle, add chicken, and brown on all sides. Add onion and garlic and cook 5 minutes longer. Add 2 tomatoes, reserved marinade, bay leaf, oregano, thyme, and chiles. Simmer, covered, 30 minutes. Add carrots, potatoes, olives, remaining 2 tomatoes, prunes, bananas, and sugar. Simmer 1 hour longer. Serve with rice and garnish with avocado slices, if desired.

Makes 4 to 6 servings

French Nutty Chicken Salad

>   2 cooked chickens
>   2 cups chopped celery
>   ½ cup chopped green pepper
>   1 tablespoon grated onion
>   4 large pimiento-stuffed olives, sliced
>   1 teaspoon salt
>   ½ teaspoon pepper
>   1 grapefruit, pared and sectioned
>   1 tablespoon Worcestershire sauce
>   Dash tabasco sauce
>   1 cup chopped pecans or almonds, boiled
>   4 hard-cooked eggs, chopped
>   ⅔–1 cup mayonnaise
>   Paprika, sliced olives, avocado, tomato wedges, or
>   parsley for garnish
>   In season: seedless green grapes, halved (optional)

*Marinade:**
>   2 tablespoons wine vinegar
>   6 tablespoons olive oil

---

*Prepared French dressing may be substituted.

1 tablespoon fresh lemon juice
1 clove garlic, mashed
1 teaspoon salt
½ teaspoon pepper

Strip chicken from bones and cut into cubes. Mix marinade (or use dressing) and marinate cooked chicken several hours. Drain. Add celery, green pepper, onion, olives, salt, pepper, and grapefruit. Stir gently to combine. Add Worcestershire, tabasco, grapes, nuts, and mayonnaise. Stir gently to mix well. Garnish with paprika, sliced olives, avocado, hard-cooked eggs, tomato wedges, or parsley.
Makes 12 servings

Bangkok Curried Chicken and Fruit Salad

2 cups cooked chicken, diced
1 cup *each* shredded coconut, blanched golden
 raisins, chopped peanuts, sliced bananas, diced
 apples, and diced celery
1 cup chutney

Marinade:
½ cup mayonnaise
1 tablespoon lime or lemon juice
2 tablespoons curry powder
Salt to taste

Mix marinade and add to all other ingredients. Toss lightly and marinate in refrigerator overnight.
Makes 12 servings

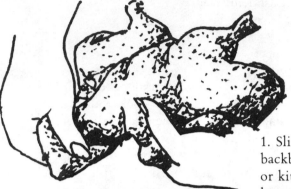

1. Slit each hen along the backbone with a meat cleaver or kitchen shears. Turn hen breast side up and pull the cut edges out to the sides. Flatten and break the breastbone by hitting it sharply with the heel of your hand or the side of the cleaver.

2. With a sharp knife, make a ¾-inch slit midway between the breastbone and legs on each side, as shown.

3. Tuck the drumsticks through the slits to secure them; the hen now becomes a *crapaud,* or toad, in appearance.

Cornish Hens à la Crapaudine

Crapaudine is a French term that refers to the method of preparing small birds, such as Cornish hens or pigeons, by splitting them down the back and trussing the wings backward under the skin (see illustrations). The bird then resembles a toad, or *crapaud*. The technique makes a practical and beautiful presentation for Cornish hens; they can be baked or barbecued. Any of the chicken marinades may be used as well as the following:

> 6 Rock Cornish hens, about 1½ pounds each
> Salt and pepper to taste

Marinade:
> ½ cup olive oil
> ¼ cup *each* sherry and vinegar
> 1 clove garlic, minced
> ½ teaspoon *each* dried thyme, sage, and basil leaves, crushed

Prepare hens as illustrated. Place hens, skin side up, in large baking dish. Sprinkle with salt and pepper. Mix marinade in a small bowl and pour over hens. Refrigerate covered, 8 hours or overnight, turning hens once. Drain. Bake covered with foil in 350° F. oven 50 minutes; remove foil and continue cooking until brown. Baste with marinade. *Or,* barbecue in covered barbecue grill with hens skin side up on rack in grill. Baste occasionally with marinade until juice is clear when a skewer is inserted in the thickest part of the leg, about 50 minutes on high heat. On uncovered grill, hens should be placed skin side down for 30 minutes and turned only once with skin up for the final cooking.
Makes 6 servings

Grilled Turkey Wings

6 turkey wings

Marinade:
¼ cup lime juice
1 clove garlic, crushed
¼ teaspoon thyme
Salt and pepper to taste
2 tablespoons oil

Cut off wing tips and reserve for making broth. Cut apart remaining 2 joints of wings. Place in a shallow dish and add lime juice, garlic, thyme, salt, and pepper. Toss to mix well. Cover and marinate at least 30 minutes. Drain wing pieces and place on greased grill. Brush with oil and grill until lightly browned. Turn and grill other side. Brush occasionally with the marinade and/or more oil. Continue to grill over glowing coals until meat in thickest portion of wing sections is tender, about 1 hour total cooking time.
Makes 6 servings

Teriyaki Turkey

1 turkey hindquarter

Marinade:
1½ cups soy sauce
½ cup lemon juice
1¼ teaspoons ginger
2 cloves garlic, minced
¼ cup minced parsley

Place turkey hindquarter in a shallow dish. Mix marinade and pour over turkey. Turn to coat well. Cover and marinate in refrigerator several hours or overnight. Drain. Grill over glowing coals until tender and browned, 1½ to 2 hours. Turn and baste with marinade as necessary to prevent burning.

When turkey feels tender when pressed, cut into the thigh joint. If no red juices run, the turkey is done. Slice across thigh and lengthwise on drumstick to serve.

Makes 3 to 4 servings

8
Fish Entrées

Fish fillets and shellfish, especially flavorful when added to marinades, are easy to prepare in the oven or on the grill. White wines, lemon and lime juices, and the same flavorings normally associated with fish are used in the marinades. The added liquids help prevent delicate fish from drying out during the cooking process.

Fresh fish fillets are preferable, though frozen fish that has been thawed and patted dry may be used. Frozen fish tends to become softer than fresh fish and is more likely to slip off the skewers in kabob recipes. To secure fish pieces, thread them alternately with foods such as zucchini rounds, tomatoes, green pepper, pineapple chunks, and so forth.

When you select fresh fish, keep in mind that it should not have a typical fishy smell. That smell suggests unfresh fish. Fresh fish should be firm. If the head is on the fish when it is purchased, the eyes should be prominent rather than shrunken, and the area behind the gills should be very red.

When you unwrap the fish at home, do not rinse it under running water; instead, fill a pan with a solution of 1 quart water and 1 tablespoon lemon juice and rinse the fish in that. Then pat dry. Prepare the marinade and let the fish soak for only an hour or two, refrigerated and covered.

Fish is already tender and delicate, so it does not require the lengthy marinating times that meats and poultry need. If the marinade does not cover the fish, either turn the fish over once during the marinating time or baste the marinade over the fish.

The greatest danger in preparing fish is overcooking it. Uncooked fish is translucent; the second it loses this translucency and becomes opaque, it is done. The only accurate way of testing is to flake the thickest part with a fork or toothpick to check the color and texture. If a recipe calls for 10 minutes of cooking time, check it at 5 and watch it carefully.

Generally, fish experts suggest a ratio of 10 minutes to each inch of thickness for broiling/grilling time. Measure the thickest part of the fish with a ruler. A whole salmon that measures 4 inches at the thickest point will broil for 40 minutes. A 1½-inch-thick halibut steak requires approximately 15 minutes total or 7½ minutes per side. But always check it before then.

BASIC MARINADES FOR FISH

Portuguese Lemon Marinade

Use this marinade for baked or broiled whole fish, thick fish fillets, or fish steaks such as albacore, greyfish, snapper, yellowtail, and tuna.

> 6 tablespoons salad oil or olive oil
> Juice and grated rind of 1 lemon
> 3 tablespoons vinegar
> ¼ cup parsley sprigs, chopped

2 green onions, chopped
1 teaspoon salt
½ teaspoon crushed peppercorns or white pepper
⅛ teaspoon thyme

Combine ingredients and place over fish in a shallow dish. Cover and refrigerate for 2 to 4 hours.
Makes ¾ cup

Teriyaki Marinade

Use this recipe with whole fish, fillets, fish steaks, and shellfish.

6 tablespoons soy sauce
6 tablespoons water or white wine
2 garlic cloves, crushed
¼ cup fresh lime juice

Mix soy sauce, water or wine, and garlic. Add the fish or shellfish. Use the lime juice to baste the food while cooking.
Makes ¾ cup

Hawaiian Marinade

Use this marinade for fish fillets.

1 cup pineapple juice or syrup drained from 1 13½-
    ounce can pineapple chunks (chunks may be
    used for a kabob recipe)
¼ cup salad oil
1 1½-ounce envelope dried spaghetti sauce mix

Combine ingredients and marinate fish fillets 1 to 2 hours. Drain marinade and use for basting.
Makes 1½ cups

Beer Marinade for Shellfish

½ cup vegetable oil
2 cups beer
2 tablespoons lemon juice
1 medium onion, sliced thin
1 garlic clove, halved
1½ teaspoons salt
¼ teaspoon pepper

Mix ingredients and pour over shelled and deveined shrimp or other shellfish. Marinate in refrigerator 2 to 3 hours.
Makes 2 cups

Dieter's Low Calorie Marinade

¾ cup instant chicken broth
6 tablespoons lemon juice
1 tablespoon fennel seeds or celery seeds
½ teaspoon ground coriander or crushed tarragon
Salt and pepper to taste

Mix all ingredients and pour over fish. Let stand, covered, 1 to 2 hours. Turn occasionally.
Makes ¾ cup for about 1 pound fish

Broiled Halibut Steaks with Sake

The following procedure may be used for preparing any fish steaks.

2 halibut steaks, 1 inch thick
Oil or butter
Marinade:
6 tablespoons olive oil
6 tablespoons sake or dry white wine
2 tablespoons lime or lemon juice
2 small garlic cloves, finely chopped

1 teaspoon *each* dried basil and freshly ground black
    pepper
1½ teaspoons salt

Combine marinade ingredients and place fish in a single layer in a flat glass dish. Pour marinade over steaks and marinate 2 hours, turning them in the marinade 2 or 3 times. Line a broiler pan or rack with foil and oil or butter the foil. Remove steaks from marinade and place on foil. Broil 4 inches from heat, about 5 minutes on each side or until done, brushing with marinade during cooking.
Makes 4 servings

Sesame Marinade for Fish Fillets

1½ pounds fish fillets in slices or large pieces for
    broiling, or 1-inch cubes for skewering

Marinade:
    ¼ cup oil
    ⅓ cup lemon juice
    1 tablespoon grated lemon peel
    1 tablespoon soy sauce
    4 teaspoons sugar
    2 tablespoons *each* toasted sesame seeds and
        chopped parsley
    ½ teaspoon salt

Mix marinade ingredients and pour over fish. Marinate 1 hour. Remove from marinade and broil or grill.

Fried Scallops

1 pound scallops
Salt, celery salt, and pepper to taste
2 eggs, beaten
Bread crumbs

Marinade:
    ¼ cup olive oil
    ¼ cup dry sherry
    2 tablespoons lemon juice

Dressing:
    ¼ cup chili sauce
    ¾ cup mayonnaise
    2 teaspoons red wine vinegar
    Deep fat for frying

If scallops are large, cut each into 3 or 4 pieces. Wash scallops well and drain on paper towels. Mix marinade and let scallops soak for ½ hour. Drain well. Sprinkle with salt, celery salt, and pepper. Dip scallops in beaten eggs, then in bread crumbs, coating thoroughly. Chill until ready to serve. For dressing stir chili sauce into mayonnaise until well blended; stir in vinegar. Chill.

Heat deep fat to 370° F. Fry scallops until medium brown. Pass dressing separately. May be used as an appetizer or an entrée.

Makes 4 to 6 servings

Tuna Fish-Pineapple Toss

    1 13½-ounce can water-packed tuna fish
    1 4-ounce can pineapple chunks in natural syrup
    Lettuce
    Mint leaves, tomatoes, and other vegetables as
        desired for garnish

Marinade:
    ¼ cup salad oil
    3 tablespoons tarragon vinegar
    3 tablespoons juice from canned pineapples
    ½ teaspoon ground cloves
    1 tablespoon crème de menthe, or fresh mint
        leaves, or 1 teaspoon mint extract

Drain tuna fish. Mix marinade and pour over tuna; stir to absorb. Cover and refrigerate 4 to 6 hours. Remove from marinade with slotted spoon. Drain pineapple chunks and gently mix into tuna. Serve on bed of lettuce garnished with mint leaves, tomatoes, and other vegetables in season.

Makes 2 to 3 servings

Barbecued Garlic Shrimp

    1 pound large raw shrimp

Marinade:
    1 cup white wine
    1 tablespoon chili sauce
    1 lime or lemon, sliced
    2 cloves garlic, minced
    ½ teaspoon *each* salt, pepper, and paprika
    Dash oregano
    Dash hot pepper sauce or tabasco

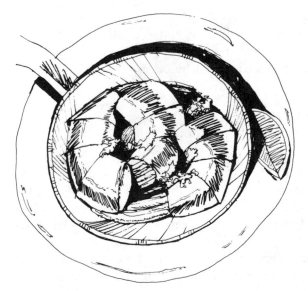

To prepare shrimp: Cut heads off with a very sharp knife; slice down the back and remove black vein by rinsing shrimp under cold running water. Leave the shell and tail on.

Mix marinade ingredients and marinate shrimp for 1 hour or more. Remove from marinade and broil in pan in oven or over charcoal fire, turning and basting often. *Or,* bake in 300° F. oven for about 30 minutes. Baste shrimp often with sauce during cooking.
Makes 4 servings

Dilled Shrimp Kabobs

 18 jumbo shrimp (about 2 pounds)
 6 small lemons
 2 large green peppers, seeded and cut into 1-inch
  squares
 12 mushrooms, halved
 Snipped fresh dill
 Cooked rice

Marinade:
 1 cup olive oil or vegetable oil
 ¼ cup cider vinegar
 2 tablespoons lemon juice
 ½ cup snipped fresh dill
 2 cloves garlic, crushed
 2 teaspoons Dijon-style mustard
 1 tablespoon snipped fresh parsley

Prepare shrimp as for Barbecued Garlic Shrimp, above. Mix marinade, pour over shrimp in bowl, and marinate overnight in refrigerator. Drain. Cut a thin slice off one end of each lemon and thread one lemon lengthwise onto each of 6 skewers. Alternate pieces of green pepper, mushrooms, and shrimp on each skewer with a green pepper at end to anchor shrimp. Grill, uncovered,

5 to 6 minutes with shrimp tails up. Turn skewers and test shrimp with sharp knife at center back until shrimp flesh looks opaque. Garnish with snipped dill. Serve with rice.

Makes 6 servings

Marinated Mussels, Boston Style

 2 cups dry white wine
 ½ cup minced green onions
 8 sprigs parsley
 1 bay leaf
 ¼ teaspoon dried thyme leaves
 ⅛ teaspoon white peppercorns
 4 quarts scrubbed mussels, soaked in 3 or 4 changes
     of cold water
 2 tablespoons lemon juice
 Lettuce

Marinade:
 ¼ cup vegetable oil or olive oil
 1 tablespoon dry vermouth
 3 tablespoons snipped fresh chives
 1 tablespoon snipped fresh parsley
 ¼ teaspoon *each* salt and white pepper

Heat wine, green onions, parsley, bay leaf, thyme, and peppercorns to boiling in large pot over high heat. Add mussels and heat to boiling. Cover and steam 2 minutes.

Uncover and stir until shells open, about 5 minutes. Discard unopened mussels. Shell mussels; transfer to large bowl and discard shells. Strain liquid from pot through coffee filters or double layer of cheesecloth into large enamel or stainless steel saucepan; add lemon juice. Cook sauce over medium heat for about 20 minutes or until it is reduced to about 1 cup. Add marinade ingredients and pour over mussels. Refrigerate, covered, stirring occasionally, about 2 hours or until cold. Transfer to lettuce-lined bowl.
Makes 4 to 6 servings

Northwest Fish Steak Grill

> 2 pounds fresh or frozen salmon, halibut, or other fish steaks

Marinade:
> 1 cup dry vermouth
> ¾ cup oil
> ⅓ cup lemon juice
> 2 tablespoons chopped chives
> 2 teaspoons salt
> 1 clove garlic, finely chopped
> ¼ teaspoon *each* marjoram, pepper, and thyme
> ⅛ teaspoon *each* sage and hot pepper sauce

Thaw steaks, if frozen. Cut into serving-size portions and place in a single layer in a shallow baking dish. Combine marinade ingredients and pour over fish. Place fish, covered, in refrigerator 4 hours, turning occasionally. Remove fish and reserve sauce for basting. Place fish on well-greased hinged wire grills. Cook about 4 inches from moderately hot coals for 8 minutes. Baste with sauce. Turn and cook 7 to 10 minutes longer, or until fish flakes easily when tested with a fork.
Makes 6 servings

Swordfish with Tomato Sauce

2 pounds swordfish (greyfish)

Marinade:
¼ cup oil
2 tablespoons lemon juice
2 teaspoons Worcestershire sauce
¼ cup minced onion
2 cloves garlic, crushed
2 teaspoons sugar
¼ teaspoon pepper

Mix marinade and pour over fish. Marinate 1 hour, turning occasionally. Drain fish, reserving marinade for basting. Broil or grill fish 5 inches from heat 15 to 20 minutes on each side or until it flakes easily with fork.
Makes 6 servings

9
Desserts

Fresh fruits marinated in the juices of other fruits or in brandies and liqueurs are tantalizing taste treats at the end of any meal. They are also between-meal tempters. Some purists argue that the fruit itself is delicious enough without any additions, but soaking fruits in zesty marinades is favored by an overwhelming majority of dessert connoisseurs.

The possible combinations are infinite. You can be as creative as you dare in the dishes you prepare, because almost any fruit can be combined with any other and all can be combined in the marinades.

Once you have tasted these delectable desserts, you can wed the fruits and their liquids with cakes and puddings or spoon the mashed fruits that have been soaked in the liquids over cobblers and ice creams.

Fruits do not require oils and vinegars in the marinades as do entrées and vegetables. The words *steeping* or *macerating*, rather than *marinating*, will be found in many cookbooks. Regardless of the term, the procedure is the same and the results are incredible.

Marinated fruits may be eaten as they come from the refrigerator and steeping liquid. They can be placed on skewers and grilled as a kabob or fried as fritters (beignets).

Liqueurs (Chapter 10), a fruit marinade themselves, may also be used as the marinade solution for other fruits.

Basic Fruit Juice Marinade

½ cup orange or other fresh fruit juice
Grated rind and juice of ½ lemon
¼ cup maple or corn syrup
1 vanilla bean or 6 coriander seeds, crushed
¼ cup brandy or liqueur (optional)

Thoroughly mix all ingredients and pour the juice over fresh fruit that has been peeled and sliced, diced, or quartered. Marinate, covered, 4 hours in the refrigerator, gently mixing and stirring occasionally. Let stand at room temperature about 20 minutes before serving.

Marinated Strawberries

    4 cups whole fresh strawberries
    ½ cup confectioners sugar
    1½ ounces *each* vodka, triple sec, and rum
    Whipped cream

Wash and hull the strawberries and toss with sugar. Mix the spirits and pour over the strawberries in a bowl. Chill at least 1 hour. Serve with whipped cream.
Makes 6 to 8 servings

Macedoine of Fresh Fruits

    1½ cups fresh fruit in season
    2 tablespoons wine or any flavor liqueur

Fruit marinated in wine or liqueur can be created in an infinite variety of combinations. The fruit should be top of the season, ripe, perfect, pared, and seeded. Favorites are strawberries, raspberries, plums, seedless green grapes, peaches, apricots, avocado slices, orange and grapefruit sections, melon balls, cherries, and nectarines. Prick fruits to allow the wine or liqueur to soak in at least 1 hour. Raw apples and pears require longer marinating periods than softer fruits.

    Some suggested combinations: oranges marinated in cognac; cherries marinated in brandy; peaches studded with cloves, marinated in mint liqueur; and melon balls with port wine.

    A macedoine is usually served cold, but you may flambé it if the fruit is at room temperature.
Makes 4 servings

Spiced Orange Slices MacKechnie

   6 oranges, peeled and sliced about ¼ inch thick
   ½ cup raisins (optional)
   Whipped cream

Marinade:
   ½ cup sugar
   1 cup burgundy or claret
   1 vanilla bean
   1 stick cinnamon
   12 whole cloves
   1 lemon, sliced thin

Mix together, then bring all marinade ingredients to a boil and simmer 15 minutes. Remove lemon and spices and pour sauce over the sliced oranges and raisins. Marinate, refrigerated, for 24 hours. Baste occasionally. Serve with whipped cream.
Makes 4 to 6 servings

Marinated Fruit with Whipped Cream Custard

> 2 cups fresh fruit in season (pineapple, pears, peaches, plums, or a mixture), cut into cubes

Marinade:

> ¼ cup fruit-flavored liqueur (kirsch, orange, peach, etc.)
> 2 tablespoons sugar

Whipped Cream Custard Sauce:
> 2 cups sifted confectioners sugar
> 1 cup milk
> 6 tablespoons butter or margarine
> 4 egg yolks, beaten
> 2 teaspoons vanilla extract
> 1 teaspoon fruit-flavored liqueur as in basic marinade for fruit (page 138)
> ½ cup heavy cream, whipped

Sprinkle fruit with liqueur and sugar and marinate 4 hours, covered, in refrigerator. Turn often so marinade permeates fruit.

For sauce: combine sugar and milk in a saucepan over medium heat. Add butter and stir until melted. Stir 2 tablespoons of hot mixture into egg yolks, then add yolks to the hot milk mixture, stirring until mixture thickens. Cool and refrigerate 3 to 4 hours. Just before serving, stir vanilla into custard and add liqueur to taste; fold into the whipped cream. Place fruits in individual dessert dishes and spoon whipped cream custard on top.

Makes 4 to 5 servings

Honey and Wine Berry Marinade

½ cup orange honey
½ cup sweet sherry or orange juice
2 cups berries (strawberries, raspberries,
    blueberries)

Combine honey with sherry or orange juice. Pour over prepared fruit and marinate in refrigerator at least 1 hour. Serve chilled.
Makes 4 servings

Sweet Dessert Fritters (Beignets de fruits glacés)

1 pound cut-up pieces of fresh fruit (apricots,
    plums, peaches, pears, apples)
3 tablespoons sugar
¾ cup Orange Liqueur (see recipe, page 149) or
    other commercial fruit base liqueur)

Batter:

1 cup flour
½ teaspoon salt
1½ teaspoons sugar
1 egg yolk
¾ cup milk
1 egg white
Vegetable oil for deep frying

Icing:

⅓ cup confectioners sugar

Clean fruit; remove pits and seeds and cut pears, peaches, and apple into candy-size pieces. Cut apricots and plums in half. Skins may be left on. Put in a bowl and sprinkle with sugar, then with liqueur, and marinate in refrigerator 1 hour.

For batter: mix flour, salt, sugar, egg yolk, and milk thoroughly. Let stand 1 hour. Add the egg white, beaten lightly, to batter, drain the fruit, and dip pieces into the batter. Deep fry a few pieces at a time in vegetable oil at 375° F. until golden brown. Drain on paper toweling. Arrange on a baking tray. Sprinkle with sugar and glaze either in a very hot oven or under a broiler.
Makes 8 to 10 servings

Fruit Upside-Down Cake

Any fruit can be used for an upside-down cake, such as canned, sliced pineapple, plums, or peaches. They can be marinated in a liqueur ahead of time. Some of the liqueur can be used in the cake batter.

½ cup butter
1 cup light brown sugar, firmly packed
1 16-ounce can sliced pineapple, or peaches, or
   plums, drained
8 maraschino cherries, drained
¼ cup fruit liqueur (orange, apricot, or peach)
2 egg yolks
1 teaspoon lemon juice
1 cup sugar
6 tablespoons hot water
1 cup sifted flour
1½ teaspoons baking powder
¼ teaspoon salt
3 egg whites, stiffly beaten

Melt butter in a 9-inch-square pan and spread brown sugar over it. Cover with drained fruit and arrange cherries between the fruit pieces. Dribble liqueur over fruit and let stand at room temperature 1 hour. Preheat oven to 325° F.

Beat egg yolks with lemon juice until thick and lemon-colored. Add sugar gradually; slowly stir in hot water. Beat until well mixed. Sift flour with baking powder and salt. Add to mixture and mix until batter is smooth. Fold in beaten egg whites. Pour batter over fruit. Bake 45 minutes or until toothpick inserted in center comes out clean. Cool 5 minutes. Turn out on platter so fruit is on top. Serve slightly warm. If desired, a topping made of whipped cream with 1 to 2 tablespoons liqueur whipped in may be served.

Note: Packaged cake mix may be used. Substitute ¼ cup liqueur along with the liquid called for in mix.
Makes 6 to 8 servings

Tutti-Frutti

Fresh fruit "cooks" as it is marinated in alcohol and sugar in this age-old recipe that never runs out as long as you keep adding to it. The marinated fruit is usable after a couple of months, but it is best after a year's time. The fruit will turn a brownish color and produce a syrup that is excellent for soaking cakes, babas and savarins. The fruit and syrup are marvelous over ice cream, in puddings, and in other desserts.

Assemble in a large covered crock or glass container equal amounts of peeled, chunked, and seeded fresh fruit in season, sugar, and vodka. Stir thoroughly once a day during the first week. After this, the mixture will ferment and settle down. If it should begin to bubble, add 1 cup sugar and 1 cup fruit to stabilize the process. Store in a cool place and add new fruits to the mixture as they come into season. Avoid using bananas and too many citrus fruits.

10
Luscious Liqueurs

The process of making liqueurs is referred to as *macerating* or *steeping*. Actually, it is a marinating process. Fruits and spices are soaked in vodka or brandy for a short period of time, then a sweetening syrup, usually sugar and water boiled together and cooled, or honey, is added.

Liqueurs are the product of marinating. They are also used to marinate other foods because they contain both acids and flavorings. Alcohol is the preservative; the flavors combine with other marinade spices to permeate the foods that are soaked in it.

The following liqueur recipes are as easy to follow as steeping tea. The procedures are the basis for creating an incredible variety of flavored liqueurs. The most popular flavorings are offered here. They provide liqueur for serving, sipping, and also to use in marinades for beef, chicken, pork, salads, and a variety of desserts.

The strained fruits become the basis for another marinade favorite—the Fruitueur's Fantasy. They may be used in delectable dessert concoctions you can create at will. Fruitueur's Fantasy, described in the following procedure, is my version of crocked fruit.

EQUIPMENT FOR LIQUEUR MAKING

- A wide-mouth 1-gallon glass (not plastic) jar for steeping
- Glass bottles for storing (washed and sterilized in a dishwasher): beer bottles, glass Perrier bottles, or decorative liqueur or wine bottles with corks or screw-on lids
- Strainers and coffee filters, funnels

THE PROCEDURE

1. Prepare the fruit as indicated. Put it in the 1-gallon jar and pour the vodka over it so the fruit is covered. Cover tightly and steep as indicated. Turn the jar upside down and shake it gently every other day or so during the steeping time.

2. Strain the fruit from the liquid. *Note:* Save the fruit in a ceramic or glass jar. Add vodka to cover and about ½ cup sugar for each cup of fruit. Refrigerate or keep in a cool place. This becomes your Fruitueur's Fantasy. Keep adding fruit to it, either more fruit from liqueurs or fresh fruit, always adding vodka or brandy to cover and sugar to taste.

3. Strain any residual particles from the liquid using a coffee filter until the liquid is clear.

4. Prepare the sugar syrup by boiling 2 parts white sugar and 1 part water together about 5 minutes. Always cool before adding to the alcohol as heat dissipates alcohol. Whole sugar grains do not dissolve in alcohol; hence the need for sugar syrup.

A maturing time is recommended. The finished liqueurs should be stored, tightly covered, in a cool, dark place.

Orange Liqueur

This is the homemade version of Cointreau, Triple Sec, Grand Marnier, etc.

3 whole sweet oranges, cut into wedges
½ lemon, cut into wedges
2 whole cloves
3 cups vodka
2 cups sugar, boiled with 1 cup water and cooled

Place the oranges, lemon, cloves and vodka in a jar. (Vodka should cover the fruit and steep 10 days.) Strain the fruit from the vodka and filter. Add sugar syrup. Mature 3 to 4 weeks.
Makes 1 quart

Lemon-Lime Liqueur

Liqueurs based on lemons and limes are tasty by themselves, and they are particularly adaptable to marinades.

Scraped and sliced peels of 4 lemons and 4 limes
3 cups vodka
1 cup sugar syrup

Scrape the peels so none of the white remains (it can leave a bitter taste). Place the peels in vodka for 2 weeks. Filter. Add sugar syrup. *Note:* 2 teaspoons *each* lemon and lime extract may be substituted and the cooled sugar syrup added at the same time. No filtering will be necessary. Let the mixture mature about 2 weeks.
Makes 4 cups

Pineapple with Vodka Liqueur

2 cups fresh cut-up pineapple (shell removed)
¼ teaspoon pure vanilla flavoring or about 1 inch
    fresh vanilla bean, cut and split
2½ cups vodka
½ cup sugar boiled in ¼ cup water

Use a fresh ripe pineapple; be sure to remove all the eyes. Place pineapple, vanilla, and vodka in a jar and let steep about 1 week. Strain and squeeze out all the juice from the pineapple by mashing it through a strainer. Filter, then sweeten with sugar syrup and filter several times until the liquid is clear. Taste the liquid; a very sweet pineapple may have given the liqueur ample sweetness. If necessary, add sweetened pineapple juice or small quantities of sugar syrup. Mature 1 month.

Note: Reserve the pineapple and combine in the Fruitueur's Fantasy jar.
Makes 2 cups

Pineapple with Rum Liqueur

½ pound fresh ripe pineapple (about 1¼ cups),
    peeled
3 cups rum

Cut pineapple into small pieces and marinate with rum in a jar. Steep for 3 weeks. Strain and filter. Mature at least 1 month.
Makes 3 cups

SPICE LIQUEURS

Almost any combination of spices will result in a tasty liqueur. Angelica root, ginger root, caraway, rosemary, cinnamon, and other familiar flavors are the basis for commercially made liqueurs such as Anisette, Benedictine, Galliano, Grand Gruyère. They utilize the same range of spices used in marinades and, therefore, are beautifully adaptable to marinade mixtures. It is a good idea to make small batches of spice liqueur and taste them. You can then adjust a second batch to be more or less spicy. The following recipes each yield 2 cups of liqueur.

Cinnamon-Allspice

> 2-inch cinnamon stick or 1½ tablespoons ground cinnamon
> 1½ teaspoons ground coriander seed
> 2 cloves
> 1½ cups vodka or ½ vodka and ½ brandy
> ½ cup sugar boiled in ¼ cup water

Steep the spices in the alcohol for 10 days. Strain and filter. Add sugar syrup.
Makes 2 cups

Kummel-Caraway Liqueur

> 1 tablespoon caraway seed
> 1 whole clove
> 1½ cups vodka
> ½ cup sugar boiled in ¼ cup water

Crush the caraway seeds lightly; add the clove and steep in the vodka 2 weeks. Strain and filter. Add sugar syrup.
Makes 2 cups

Mint Liqueur

> 4–5 tablespoons fresh or 2 tablespoons dried well-
>   crumbled mint, peppermint, or spearmint
>   leaves, *or* 2–3 teaspoons pure mint or
>   peppermint extract
> 3 cups vodka
> 1 cup sugar boiled in ½ cup water

Steep the mint in the vodka for about 2 weeks and shake the bottle occasionally. Strain and filter. Be sure to press all the juices from the leaves with a spoon against the strainer. Strain. Add sugar water and mature 2 weeks. When using extracts, combine all ingredients, including the sugar syrup. Shake well and steep at least 24 hours, preferably a week or 2. Then add sugar water.

Note: For crème de menthe, which is sweeter, add 2 cups sugar boiled in ½ cup water.

Makes 1 quart

Rosemary Liqueur

> 1½ teaspoons rosemary leaves or 1 teaspoon ground
>   rosemary
> 1 mint leaf
> Sliced and scraped peel of ½ lemon
> ¼ teaspoon coriander
> 1½ cups vodka
> ½ cup sugar boiled with ¼ cup water

Gently crush the rosemary leaves and mint with the back of a spoon on a cutting board so the aroma and oils are released. Add the lemon and herbs to the vodka and steep for 10 days. Strain and filter. And the sugar syrup. Mature for 2 to 4 weeks.

Makes 2 cups

Appendix: Measurement Equivalents

U.S. liquid measure volume equivalents

A pinch =   Less than ⅛ teaspoon
60 drops =   1 teaspoon
1 teaspoon =   ⅓ tablespoon
1 tablespoon =   3 teaspoons or ½ ounce
2 tablespoons =   1 fluid ounce
4 tablespoons =   ¼ cup
5⅓ tablespoons =   ⅓ cup
8 tablespoons =   ½ cup or 4 ounces
16 tablespoons =   1 cup or 8 ounces
1 cup =   ½ pint or 8 fluid ounces
2 cups =   1 pint
4 cups =   32 ounces or 1 quart
1 pint liquid =   16 ounces
1 quart liquid =   2 pints or 32 ounces
1 gallon liquid =   4 quarts
⅕ gallon or
    ⅘ quart=   25.6 ounces

U.S. liquid and volume measures and metric equivalents

1 teaspoon =	5 milliliters
1 tablespoon =	15 milliliters
1 ounce =	29.5 milliliters
1 cup (8 ounces) =	237 milliliters
1 pint (16 ounces) =	473 milliliters
⅕ gallon or "fifth" =	¾ liter
1 quart =	.946 liter
½ gallon =	1.9 liters
1 gallon =	3.78 liters

Index

A

Acids, in marinades, 9
African marinated fried fish,
 38
Anise, 10
Appetizers, 19-20
 African marinated fried
  fish, 38
 brandied beef kabobs, 32
 broiled sesame chicken,
  29-30
 fruit with wine marinade,
  21
 Gravlak—Swedish
  marinated salmon,
  35-36
 Indonesian satés, 28-29
 Jicama (Yam bean), 23-24
 marinated artichoke
  hearts, 25
 marinated cocktail beets,
  24
 marinated herring, 36
 marinated mushrooms, 23

 marinated raw beef slices,
  31
 Mexican marinated fried
  fish, 37
 minted melon on skewers,
  20
 oriental chicken wing
  tidbits, 30
 peach-flavored glazed ham
  cubes, 31
 plum and bacon
  appetizers, 21-22
 raw beef sirloin cooked in
  lime juice, 32
 rosy radishes, 22-23
 rumaki, 26-27
 seviche, 20, 33
 shrimp in marinade, 38-39
 zesty shrimp, rumaki style,
  27
apple-flavored chicken
 kabobs, 114
Armenian herb lamb
 marinade, 91

Vinaigrette vegetables, 54
Vinegar, 9, 15, 16, 17

W

Wax beans
basic three-bean salad, 47
Whiskey, 15
Whiskey marinade for baked
teriyaki chicken, 113-14
Wine, 9, 15-16, 17
Wine marinades
dieter's basic for steak,
64-65
flank steak with rosé wine,
67

porterhouse steak with
zesty, 67
Whole string bean niçoise, 46

X, Y, & Z

Yam bean, 23-24
Yogurt, 16, 17
Yogurt kabob marinade with
chile pepper, 77
Zucchini
minted, 52
and mushrooms, 51-52